These Dreams Belong To

See, I am doing a new thing! Now it springs up; do you not perceive it?

Are you writer who wants to impact your world, your family and your life? Then you are about to have a brilliant year! Because we at My Book Therapy have created a planner just for you. With this planner, your epic writing year is just beginning. You will grow. You will be changed. And you will see your projects, plans and dreams happen.

I am a firm believer that the writing journey should change us. If it hasn't then we've missed the point. But you're changed not just by putting words on the page, but by the relationships you cultivate, the activities you pursue and the ways you incorporate spiritual growth into your life.

I've always struggled with how to merge my personal, family, writing and business life into one planner. I usually have four different books: a journal, a family planner, a business planner and a writing calendar. Keeping track of them all only adds to my stress. For years I yearned for something that would integrate all the essential elements of these planners into one epic planner that could capture not just my muses, but also help me plan my year, my 90-day goals, my weekly goals, my daily activities and even keep brainstorming in one place.

Wouldn't it be great if it also helped me track some of the habits I wanted to cultivate, maybe daily meals, help me keep track of my water intake and a few other things I wanted to nudge in the right direction?

And, if it could also help me plan and stay on track with my writing projects, my marketing, my growth as a writer and any other projects, that would be even better!

It might even be inspirational, with my Word and Verse of the year, some quotes to pull from, and places for weekly affirmations.

And it should be pretty.

Enter My Story Matters: The My Book Therapy 2018 planner. Dive in with the instructions below, and get ready to have a brilliant year.

Let's do this.

Susan Mayne

founder, My Book Therapy
USA Today best-selling author

I am making a way in the wilderness and streams in the wasteland.
Isaiah 43:19 New International Version (NIV)

How to use this planner

Start with your Year in Review and go through the questions. They're designed to help you curate the joy from last year and cultivate it into this year's projects.

Move onto the Plans for 2018, working through the questions to help you dream big, and put a strategy to your vision.

Then you'll get personal and look at your Word & Verse of the year. Go to the dream boards and start brainstorming what projects are blooming inside. Books, Blogs, Marketing—anything. Your dream boards and project boards are a perfect place to try out those big ideas. They are down into three sections—Writing, Marketing, and (story)Craft—the areas all writers should be growing in. But you can add more!

Then, you'll take those big projects and put them into four quarters. The easiest way to do this is to separate the projects into four big pieces you'll accomplish over the course of the year.

Now, this is where the magic of getting things done happens. Simply divide those Quarter goals into smaller, bite-sized Tasks you'll do over ninety days. We've allowed for sixteen tasks per box (in case you want to add more per week), but divide them into at least twelve smaller bites.

You'll be all set to add them, one week at a time, into your Month at a Glance!

Now, drink some hot cocoa, take out some coloring pens and start working on January. Grab your tasks for each quarter and add them to your Month at a Glance, write in all the big dates into your calendar, then every week simply add the task for that week to the Make it Happen section. We've also included a space for your daily meditation and prayers, as well as any inspirational verses.

Finally, you'll "Do it!" Your plan in action happens with the Daily Logs. Here, you'll add all those daily tasks that help you complete your 90-Day Goals...and yearly goals. Because that's how the magic happens. But you're not going to forget about the rest of your life either, those daily habits and actions that add up to an effective, even abundant life.

You might want to add one task/day per category. Or maybe you spend one week working on one category, finishing all the tasks for the month. Or maybe, like me, you create specific days for specific tasks. I like to do all my marketing and craft tasks on Mondays. (Sometimes I work ahead!) Then, I write on Tuesdays, Wednesdays and Thursdays. On Fridays I work on other projects. It's up to you, but by the end of the month, you'll have completed all your tasks and tackled a big chunk of your Quarterly projects.

All good systems have a place for analysis, so at the end of the month you'll take a good look at your wins, your challenges and plan another fabulous month. At the end of December, you'll analyze the year and think about all the things that brought joy, all the hopes for next year, and a recap the truths you've learned.

The planner also includes a place for Storycrafting – enough for three novels. With a storycrafting page that includes all the elements for sketching out your story, two Story Equation charts to create your characters, and a plotting page, you'll have all the basics for your rough outline. If you're an indie author, included is a per-book project planning sheet to keep track of all your benchmark deadlines and project finances.

Your story matters – the one you're living, as well as the one you're creating. Capture it all here and have a brilliant year!

A Year at a Glance:

January

S	M	T	W	T	F	S
	1	2	3	4	5	6
7	8	9	10	11	12	13
14	15	16	17	18	19	20
21	22	23	24	25	26	27
28	29	30	31			

Dates to remember:

February

S	M	T	W	T	F	S
				1	2	3
4	5	6	7	8	9	10
11	12	13	14	15	16	17
18	19	20	21	22	23	24
25	26	27	28			

Dates to remember:

March

S	M	T	W	T	F	S
				1	2	3
4	5	6	7	8	9	10
11	12	13	14	15	16	17
18	19	20	21	22	23	24
25	26	27	28	29	30	31

Dates to remember:

July

S	M	T	W	T	F	S
1	2	3	4	5	6	7
8	9	10	11	12	13	14
15	16	17	18	19	20	21
22	23	24	25	26	27	28
29	30	31				

Dates to remember:

August

S	M	T	W	T	F	S
				1	2	3	4
5	6	7	8	9	10	11
12	13	14	15	16	17	18
19	20	21	22	23	24	25
26	27	28	29	30	31	

Dates to remember:

September

S	M	T	W	T	F	S
						1
2	3	4	5	6	7	8
9	10	11	12	13	14	15
16	17	18	19	20	21	22
23	24	25	26	27	28	29
30						

Dates to remember:

Color code your events

☐ birthdays ☐ anniversaries ☐ holidays ☐ vacations

Project Vision

April

S	M	T	W	T	F	S
1	2	3	4	5	6	7
8	9	10	11	12	13	14
15	16	17	18	19	20	21
22	23	24	25	26	27	28
29	30					

Dates to remember:

May

S	M	T	W	T	F	S
		1	2	3	4	5
6	7	8	9	10	11	12
13	14	15	16	17	18	19
20	21	22	23	24	25	26
27	28	29	30	31		

Dates to remember:

June

S	M	T	W	T	F	S
					1	2
3	4	5	6	7	8	9
10	11	12	13	14	15	16
17	18	19	20	21	22	23
24	25	26	27	28	29	30

Dates to remember:

October

S	M	T	W	T	F	S
	1	2	3	4	5	6
7	8	9	10	11	12	13
14	15	16	17	18	19	20
21	22	23	24	25	26	27
28	29	30	31			

Dates to remember:

November

S	M	T	W	T	F	S
				1	2	3
4	5	6	7	8	9	10
11	12	13	14	15	16	17
18	19	20	21	22	23	24
25	26	27	28	29	30	

Dates to remember:

December

S	M	T	W	T	F	S
						1
2	3	4	5	6	7	8
9	10	11	12	13	14	15
16	17	18	19	20	21	22
23	24	25	26	27	28	29
30	31					

Dates to remember:

Color code your events

☐ conferences ☐ deadlines ☐ pub dates ☐ projects

Let's Start with your Dreams!

Did you have a word or verse for last year?

How did you see it playing out?

What were your biggest challenges?

What were your greatest victories?

What made the biggest impact on you...and how did it change you?

Listen carefully to your heart, and ask yourself, "What am I still dreaming about becoming or doing?"

What brings you Joy?

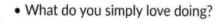

- What do you simply love doing?

- What activities do you gravitate toward in your free time?

- What would be your "dream book" to write?

in Review

How is your writing craft?

What are the top areas of the craft you feel are your strongest?

Are you a master at ONE of these skills?

What are your three weak areas?

Let's pick one to work on.

How? What books did you love last year?

Out of those books, which author excelled in the area you need work on?

What other authors will you read to learn from this year?

What book(s) or retreats will you add to your education this year? (craft, professional, etc.)

Plans for 2018

Let's talk about your novels!

What is your core message as an author?

Look through what you wrote last year (all the bodies of work).

- · What did you love best?

- · What did you struggle with? Why?

If you could rate your favorite writing projects—including genres, rank them from 1-5 (1 being your favorite).

Why were they your favorite?

What projects cost more time and energy than they were worth?

Plans for 2018

Let's take a look at the trends.

What genres or writing trends are intriguing to you? Why?

Do the new trends fit into your core message/vision statement?

Could they be adapted for the genre or projects you love?

Let's get specific.

Based on what you love and any market opportunities, what would you like to write this year? Dream BIG!!!

Plans for 2018

Let's talk about your writing habits.

How much writing time do you have?

How many words/scenes can you write in that writing session?

Now, look at your average word count per writing session, and the length of each writing session... how many words or scenes can you write/week?

How much time do you spend for professional growth and expanding your fan base?

What are the distractions that should be eliminated? (time wasters!)

Let's create a publishing strategy!

What book(s) do you want to write?

Would they be more suited to traditional or indie publishing?

Considerations:
· Series?
· One-off?
· Collection?
· Length?

What is the projected length of each book?

Could you combine two or more for a collection or series? What about a free book?

Plans for 2018

Now...Let's create a plan!

What book will you write first?

What is the projected length?

How many words can you write per writing session?

How much time do you need for each writing session?

Do the math: How many writing sessions do you need to schedule to complete your story?

Now, look at your average word count per writing session, and the length of each writing session, compare that to your free time/writing space each week.

Summary:

What will you write this year?

When will you write?

What is your deadline?

How will you grow as a writer?

How will you expand your fan base?

What will you do to get your work published?

One Word

My Word:

Why did you choose that word?

What does it mean?

One Verse

My Verse

Why did you choose this verse?

Write out a prayer for 2018.

Dreamboard: Writing
What books would you like to write this year?

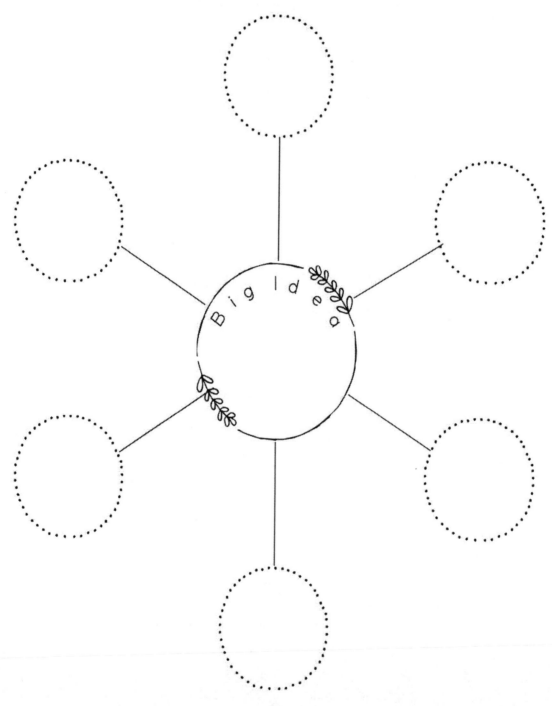

The future belongs to those who believe in the beauty of their dreams.
~Eleanor Roosevelt

Project Boards

Project	Deadline
Description	

Project	Deadline
Description	

Project	Deadline
Description	

Project	Deadline
Description	

Dreamboard: Marketing

What marketing goals would you like to achieve?

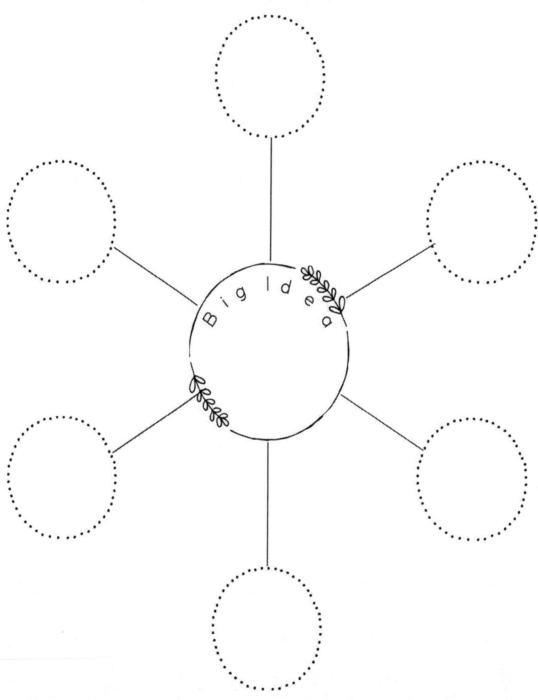

Project Boards

Project	Deadline
Description	

Project	Deadline
Description	

Project	Deadline
Description	

Project	Deadline
Description	

Dreamboard: Storycraft

What storycraft elements would you like to improve?

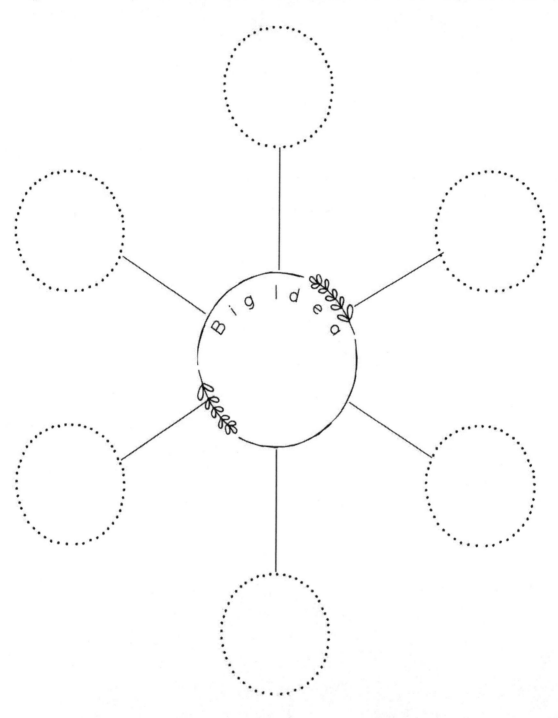

Big Idea

Project Boards

Project	Deadline
Description	

Project	Deadline
Description	

Project	Deadline
Description	

Project	Deadline
Description	

Dreamboard: Other

What other projects would you like to pursue this year?

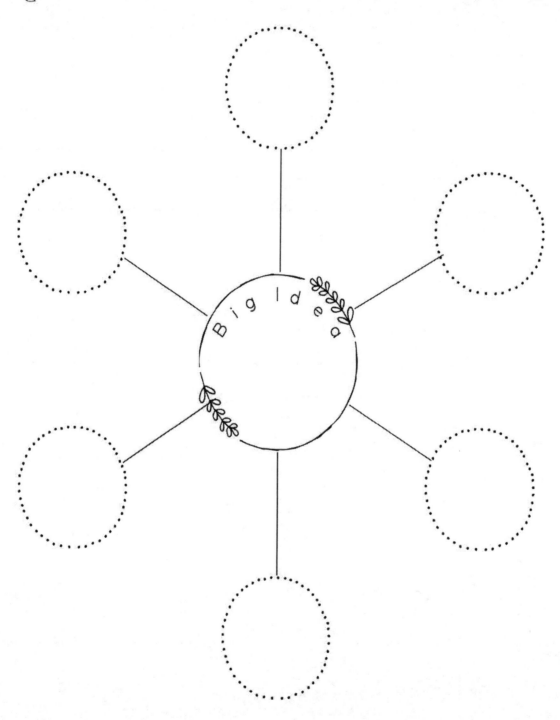

Project Boards

Project	Deadline
Description	

Project	Deadline
Description	

Project	Deadline
Description	

Project	Deadline
Description	

Quarter One Goals

"A goal properly set is halfway reached."
Zig Ziglar

January	February	March
Writing	Writing	Writing
Marketing	Marketing	Marketing
Craft	Craft	Craft
Other	Other	Other

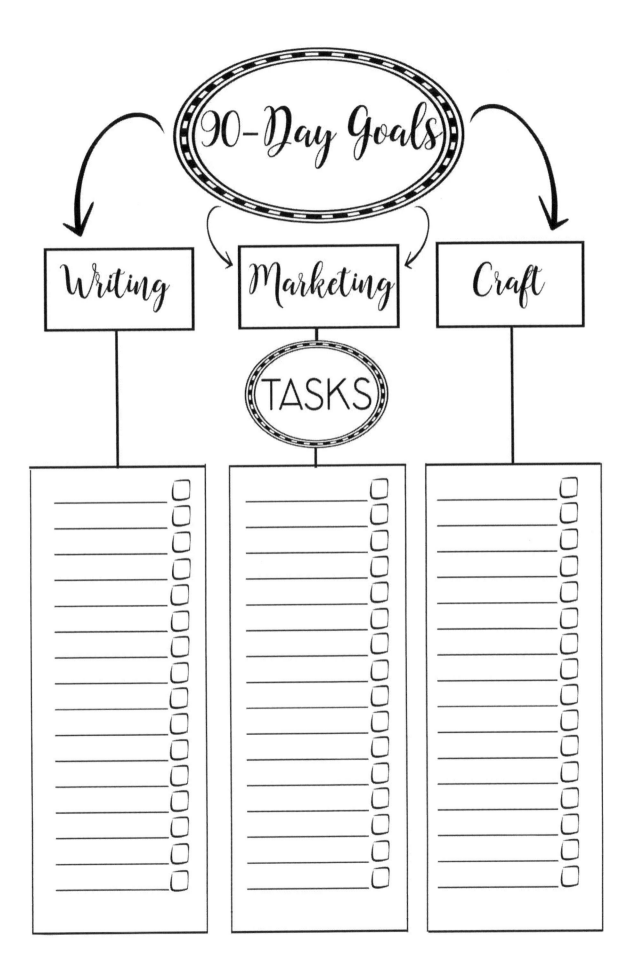

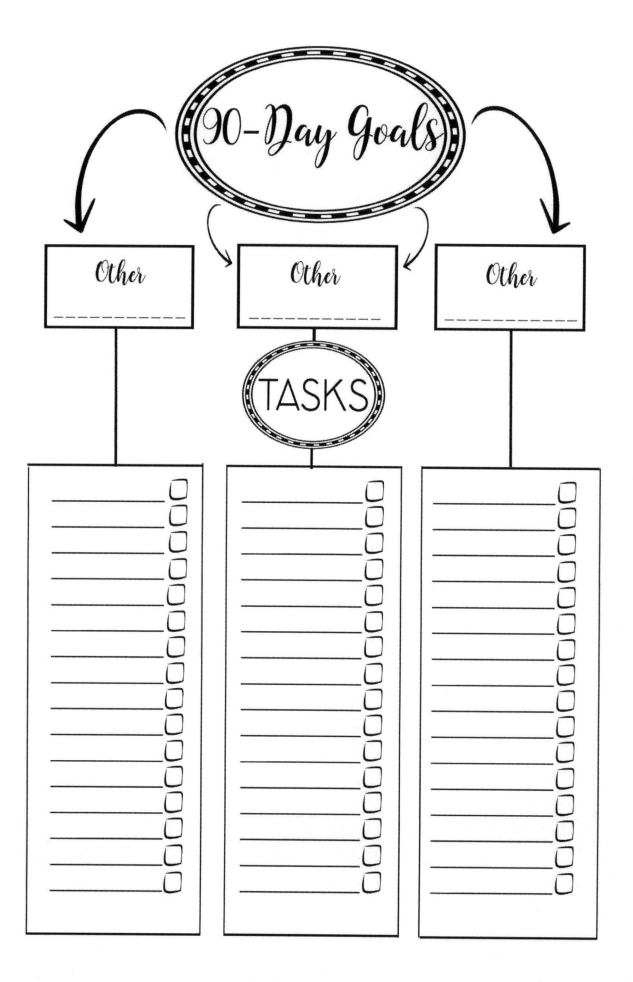

90-Day Goals

Other
___ ___ ___ ___

Other
___ ___ ___ ___

Other
___ ___ ___ ___

TASKS

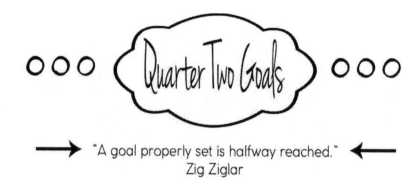

Quarter Two Goals

→ "A goal properly set is halfway reached." ←
Zig Ziglar

April	May	June
Writing	Writing	Writing
Marketing	Marketing	Marketing
Craft	Craft	Craft
Other	Other	Other

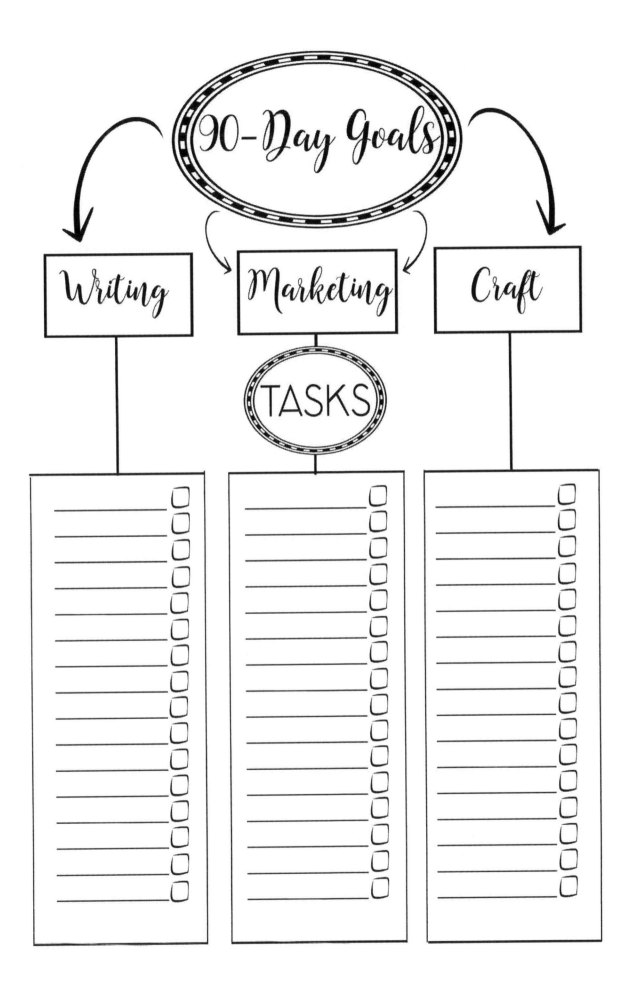

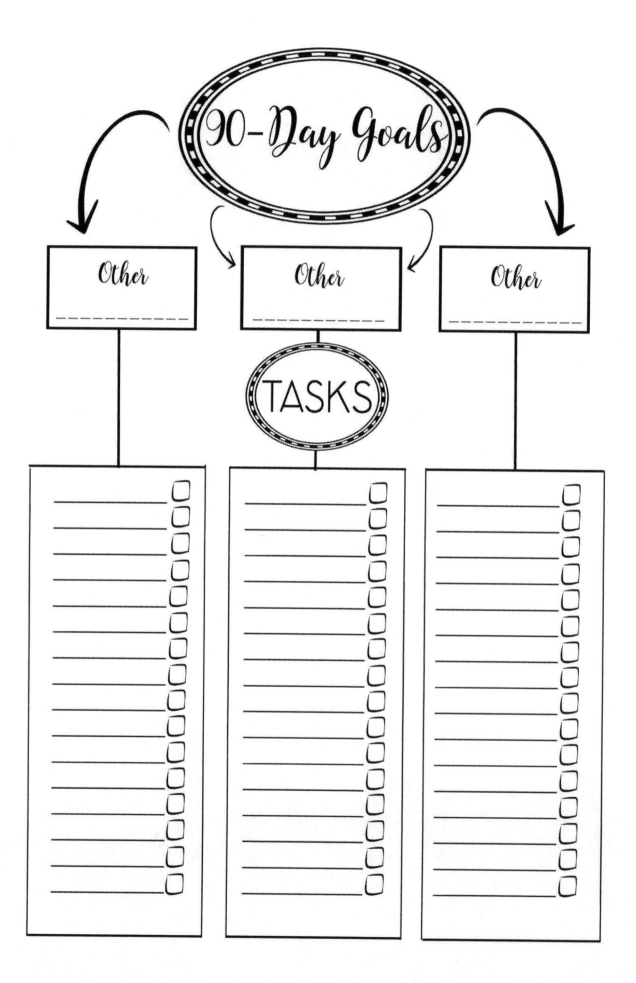

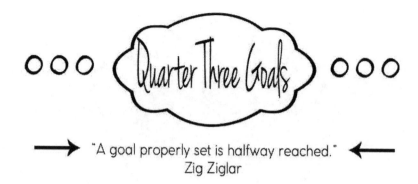

"A goal properly set is halfway reached."
Zig Ziglar

July	August	September
Writing	Writing	Writing
Marketing	Marketing	Marketing
Craft	Craft	Craft
Other	Other	Other

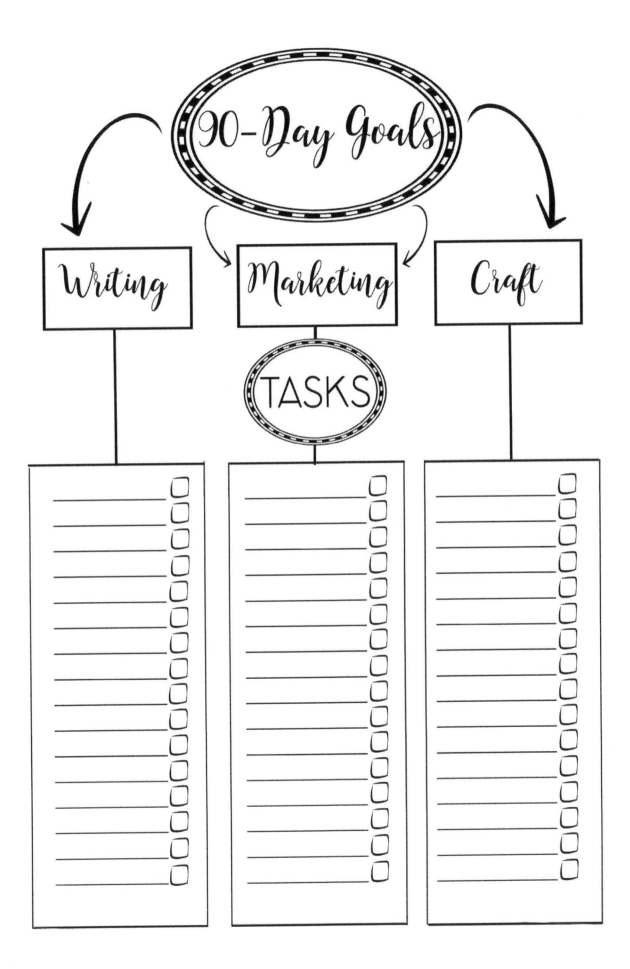

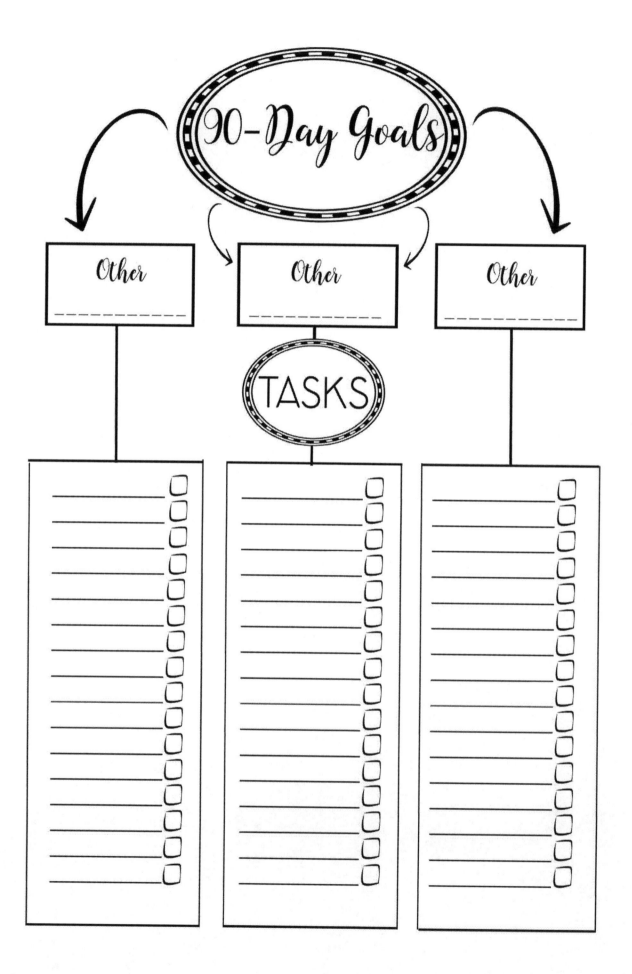

Quarter Four Goals

→ "A goal properly set is halfway reached." ←
Zig Ziglar

October	November	December
Writing	Writing	Writing
Marketing	Marketing	Marketing
Craft	Craft	Craft
Other	Other	Other

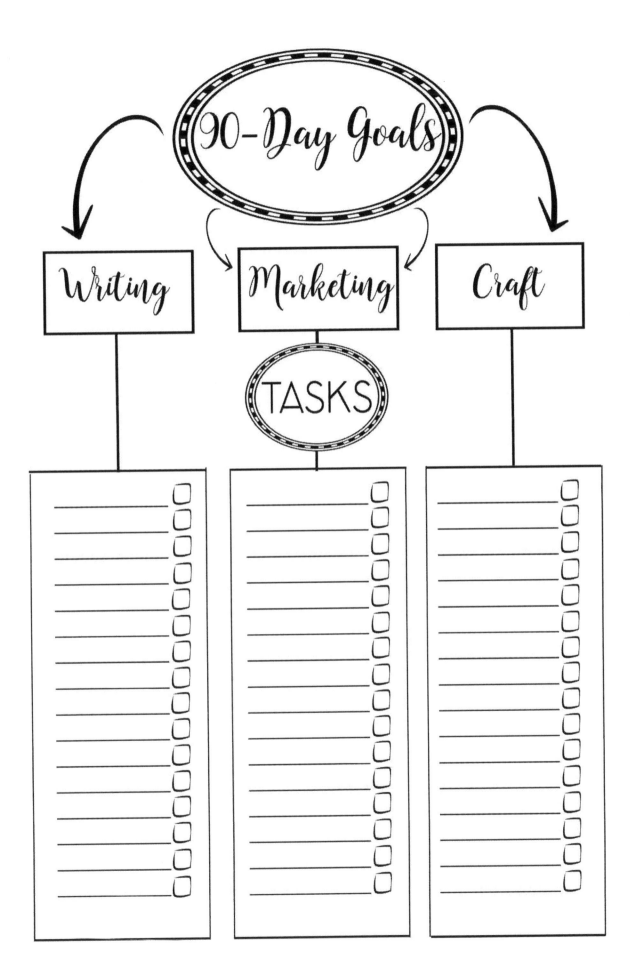

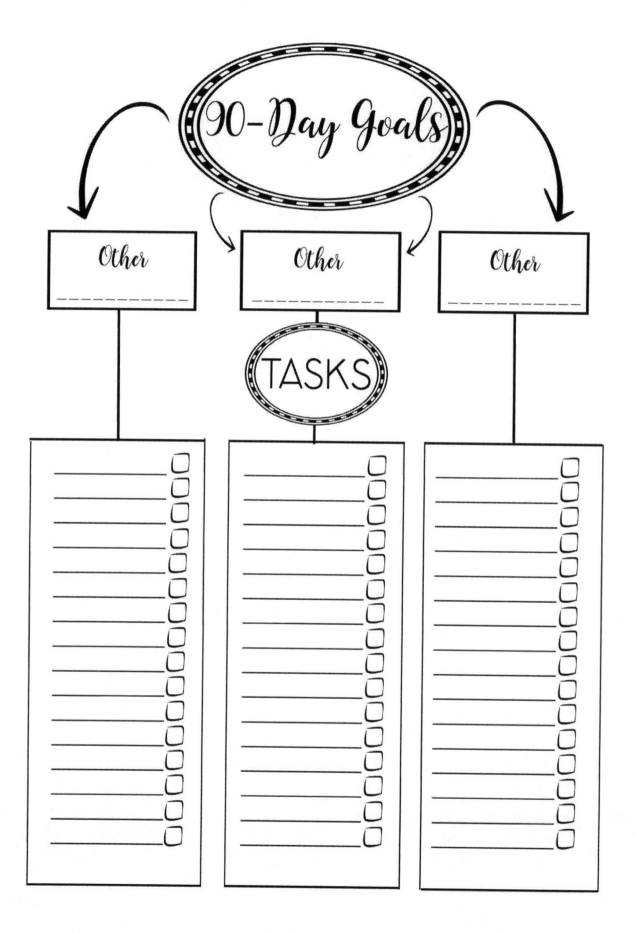

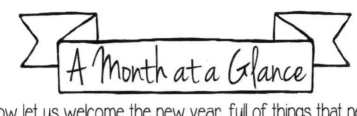

A Month at a Glance

And now let us welcome the new year, full of things that never were.
Lydia Sweatt

Goals: Writing

Week 1: _____
Week 2: _____
Week 3: _____
Week 4: _____
Week 5: _____

Goals: Marketing

Week 1: _____
Week 2: _____
Week 3: _____
Week 4: _____
Week 5: _____

Goals: Craft

Week 1: _____
Week 2: _____
Week 3: _____
Week 4: _____
Week 5: _____

Goals: Other

Week 1: _____
Week 2: _____
Week 3: _____
Week 4: _____
Week 5: _____

Important Dates

_____
_____
_____
_____
_____

Things to Remember:

_____
_____
_____
_____
_____

I AM grateful FOR:

_____
_____
_____
_____

Favorite Writing Quote

January

Sunday	Monday	Tuesday	Wednesday
	1	2	3
7	8	9	10
14	15	16	17
21	22	23	24
28	29	30	31

2018 ◇◈◇

Thursday	Friday	Saturday	Notes
4	5	6	
11	12	13	
18	19	20	
25	26	27	

Daily

Monday

Verse

Reflection

Truth

Prayers

Tuesday

Verse

Reflection

Truth

Prayers

Wednesday

Verse

Reflection

Truth

Prayers

Thursday

Verse

Reflection

Truth

Prayers

Inspiration

Friday

Verse

Reflection

Truth

Prayers

Saturday

Verse

Reflection

Truth

Prayers

Sunday

Verse

Reflection

Truth

Prayers

What encouraged you this week?

What can you do to encourage someone else?

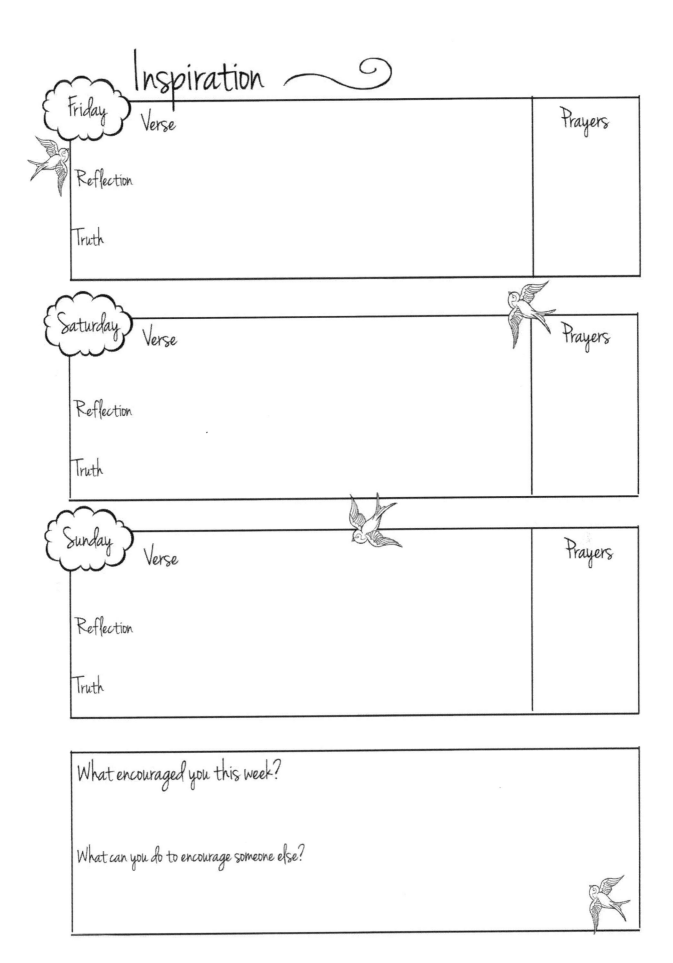

Make it

Writing
☐
☐
☐
☐
☐
☐
☐

Marketing
☐
☐
☐
☐
☐
☐
☐

Craft
☐
☐
☐
☐
☐
☐
☐

Calls to Make

Errands

Happen

Project

- ☐
- ☐
- ☐
- ☐
- ☐
- ☐
- ☐

Other

- ☐
- ☐
- ☐
- ☐
- ☐
- ☐
- ☐

Menu

Monday
Tuesday
Wednesday
Thursday
Friday
Saturday
Sunday

January

S	M	T	W	T	F	S
	1	2	3	4	5	6
7	8	9	10	11	12	13
14	15	16	17	18	19	20
21	22	23	24	25	26	27
28	29	30	31			

Do

Weekly Affirmation: _____

Monday	Tuesday	Wednesday
Dinner:	Dinner:	Dinner:
Exercise:	Exercise:	Exercise:

Notes

Water

	1	2	3	4	5	6	7	8
M								
T								
W								
T								
F								
S								
S								

It

Thursday	Friday	Saturday
		Sunday
Dinner:	Dinner:	
Exercise:	Exercise:	

Daily Habits	M	T	W	T	F	S	S

Appointments

Daily

Monday

Verse

Reflection

Truth

Prayers

Tuesday

Verse

Reflection

Truth

Prayers

Wednesday

Verse

Reflection

Truth

Prayers

Thursday

Verse

Reflection

Truth

Prayers

Inspiration

Friday

Verse

Reflection

Truth

Prayers

Saturday

Verse

Reflection

Truth

Prayers

Sunday

Verse

Reflection

Truth

Prayers

What encouraged you this week?

What can you do to encourage someone else?

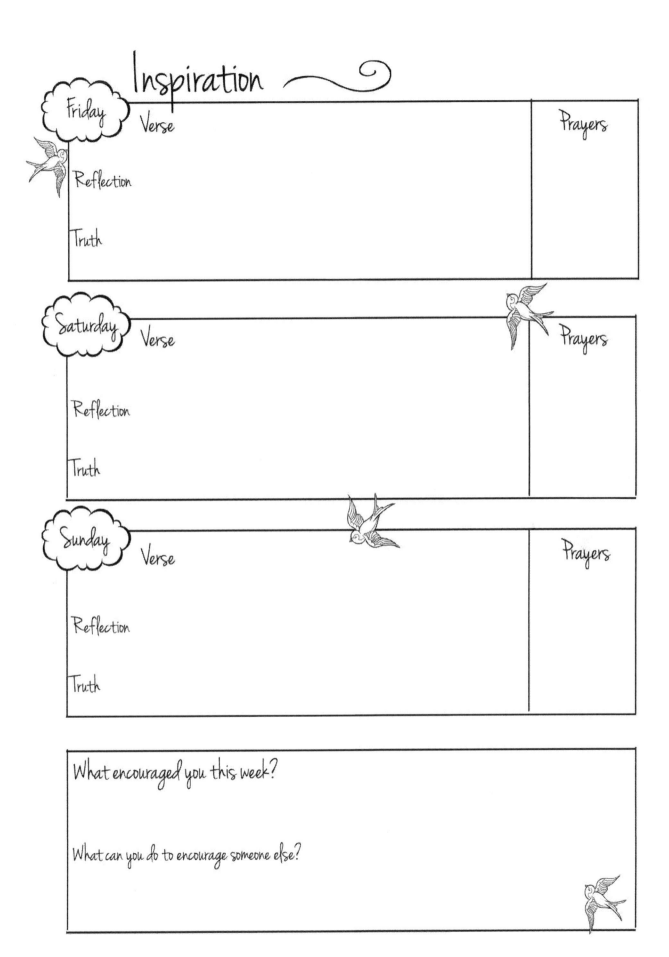

Make it

Writing

☐
☐
☐
☐
☐
☐
☐

Marketing

☐
☐
☐
☐
☐
☐
☐

Craft

☐
☐
☐
☐
☐
☐
☐

Calls to Make

Errands

Happen

Project

- ☐
- ☐
- ☐
- ☐
- ☐
- ☐
- ☐

Other

- ☐
- ☐
- ☐
- ☐
- ☐
- ☐
- ☐

Menu

Monday
Tuesday
Wednesday
Thursday
Friday
Saturday
Sunday

January

S	M	T	W	T	F	S
	1	2	3	4	5	6
7	8	9	10	11	12	13
14	15	16	17	18	19	20
21	22	23	24	25	26	27
28	29	30	31			

Do

Weekly Affirmation: _____

Monday	Tuesday	Wednesday
Dinner:	Dinner:	Dinner:
Exercise:	Exercise:	Exercise:

Notes

Water

	1	2	3	4	5	6	7	8
M								
T								
W								
T								
F								
S								
S								

It - - - - - - - - - - - ➤

Thursday	Friday	Saturday

Dinner: Dinner:

Exercise: Exercise:

Sunday

Daily Habits

	M	T	W	T	F	S	S

Appointments

Daily

Monday

Verse

Reflection

Truth

Prayers

Tuesday

Verse

Reflection

Truth

Prayers

Wednesday

Verse

Reflection

Truth

Prayers

Thursday

Verse

Reflection

Truth

Prayers

Inspiration

Friday

Verse

Prayers

Reflection

Truth

Saturday

Verse

Prayers

Reflection

Truth

Sunday

Verse

Prayers

Reflection

Truth

What encouraged you this week?

What can you do to encourage someone else?

Make it

Writing

☐

☐

☐

☐

☐

☐

☐

Marketing

☐

☐

☐

☐

☐

☐

☐

Craft

☐

☐

☐

☐

☐

☐

☐

Calls to Make

Errands

Happen

Project

- ☐
- ☐
- ☐
- ☐
- ☐
- ☐
- ☐

Other

- ☐
- ☐
- ☐
- ☐
- ☐
- ☐

Menu

Monday
Tuesday
Wednesday
Thursday
Friday
Saturday
Sunday

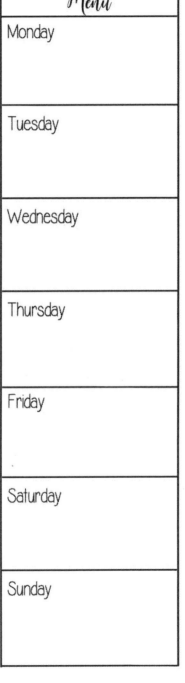

January

S	M	T	W	T	F	S
	1	2	3	4	5	6
7	8	9	10	11	12	13
14	15	16	17	18	19	20
21	22	23	24	25	26	27
28	29	30	31			

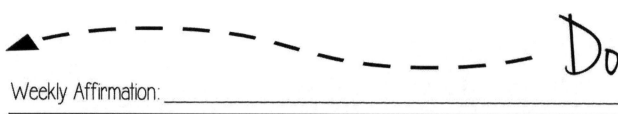

Weekly Affirmation: _____

Monday	Tuesday	Wednesday
Dinner:	Dinner:	Dinner:
Exercise:	Exercise:	Exercise:

Notes

	1	2	3	4	5	6	7	8
M								
T								
W								
T								
F								
S								
S								

Water

It

Thursday	Friday	Saturday

Sunday

Dinner:

Exercise:

Dinner:

Exercise:

Daily Habits	M	T	W	T	F	S	S

Appointments

Daily

Monday

Verse

Reflection

Truth

Prayers

Tuesday

Verse

Reflection

Truth

Prayers

Wednesday

Verse

Reflection

Truth

Prayers

Thursday

Verse

Reflection

Truth

Prayers

Inspiration

Friday

Verse

Reflection

Truth

Prayers

Saturday

Verse

Reflection

Truth

Prayers

Sunday

Verse

Reflection

Truth

Prayers

What encouraged you this week?

What can you do to encourage someone else?

Make it

Writing

- ☐
- ☐
- ☐
- ☐
- ☐
- ☐
- ☐

Marketing

- ☐
- ☐
- ☐
- ☐
- ☐
- ☐
- ☐

Craft

- ☐
- ☐
- ☐
- ☐
- ☐
- ☐
- ☐

Calls to Make

Errands

Happen

Project

- ☐
- ☐
- ☐
- ☐
- ☐
- ☐
- ☐

Other

- ☐
- ☐
- ☐
- ☐
- ☐
- ☐

Menu

Monday
Tuesday
Wednesday
Thursday
Friday
Saturday
Sunday

January

S	M	T	W	T	F	S
	1	2	3	4	5	6
7	8	9	10	11	12	13
14	15	16	17	18	19	20
21	22	23	24	25	26	27
28	29	30	31			

Do

Weekly Affirmation: _____

Monday	Tuesday	Wednesday
Dinner:	Dinner:	Dinner:
Exercise:	Exercise:	Exercise:

Notes

Water

	1	2	3	4	5	6	7	8
M								
T								
W								
T								
F								
S								
S								

It

Thursday	Friday	Saturday
		Sunday
Dinner:	Dinner:	
Exercise:	Exercise:	

Daily Habits

	M	T	W	T	F	S	S

Appointments

Daily

Monday
Verse

Reflection

Truth

Prayers

Tuesday
Verse

Reflection

Truth

Prayers

Wednesday
Verse

Reflection

Truth

Prayers

Thursday
Verse

Reflection

Truth

Prayers

Inspiration

Friday

Verse

Reflection

Truth

Prayers

Saturday

Verse

Reflection

Truth

Prayers

Sunday

Verse

Reflection

Truth

Prayers

What encouraged you this week?

What can you do to encourage someone else?

Make it

Writing

- [ ]
- [ ]
- [ ]
- [ ]
- [ ]
- [ ]
- [ ]

Marketing

- [ ]
- [ ]
- [ ]
- [ ]
- [ ]
- [ ]
- [ ]

Craft

- [ ]
- [ ]
- [ ]
- [ ]
- [ ]
- [ ]
- [ ]

Calls to Make

Errands

Happen

Project

- ☐
- ☐
- ☐
- ☐
- ☐
- ☐
- ☐

Other

- ☐
- ☐
- ☐
- ☐
- ☐
- ☐

Menu

Monday	
Tuesday	
Wednesday	
Thursday	
Friday	
Saturday	
Sunday	

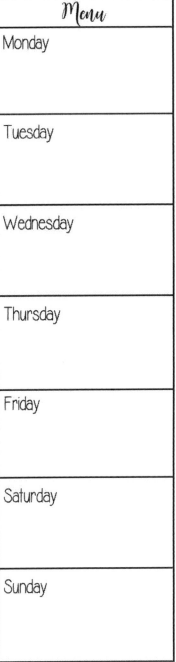

January

S	M	T	W	T	F	S
	1	2	3	4	5	6
7	8	9	10	11	12	13
14	15	16	17	18	19	20
21	22	23	24	25	26	27
28	29	30	31			

Do

Weekly Affirmation: _____

Monday	Tuesday	Wednesday
Dinner:	Dinner:	Dinner:
Exercise:	Exercise:	Exercise:

Notes

	1	2	3	4	5	6	7	8
M								
T								
W								
T								
F								
S								
S								

Water

It

Thursday	Friday	Saturday

Dinner:

Dinner:

Exercise:

Exercise:

Sunday

Daily Habits

	M	T	W	T	F	S	S

Appointments

Monthly Review

→ Best ←

Accomplishments	Significant Events	What brought the most joy?

← Worst →

Biggest Challenges	Personal Struggles	Changes for Next Month

Truth:

How am I different?

Financial Tracker

Income	
Expenses	
Profit	
Tithe	
Savings	

Weight Tracker

	M	T	W	T	F
Week 1					
Week 2					
Week 3					
Week 4					
Week 5					

Books I Read

I am most proud of:

Ideas & inspiration for next month

A Month at a Glance

And now let us welcome the new year, full of things that never were.
Lydia Sweatt

Goals: Writing

Week 1: _____
Week 2: _____
Week 3: _____
Week 4: _____
Week 5: _____

Goals: Marketing

Week 1: _____
Week 2: _____
Week 3: _____
Week 4: _____
Week 5: _____

Goals: Craft

Week 1: _____
Week 2: _____
Week 3: _____
Week 4: _____
Week 5: _____

Goals: Other

Week 1: _____
Week 2: _____
Week 3: _____
Week 4: _____
Week 5: _____

Important Dates

_____
_____
_____
_____

Things to Remember:

_____
_____
_____
_____

I AM grateful FOR:

_____
_____
_____

Favorite Writing Quote

February

Sunday	Monday	Tuesday	Wednesday
4	5	6	7
11	12	13	14
18	19	20	21
25	26	27	28

2018 ◇ ◆ ◇

Thursday	Friday	Saturday	Notes
4	5	6	
11	12	13	
18	19	20	
25	26	27	

Daily

Monday

Verse

Reflection

Truth

Prayers

Tuesday

Verse

Reflection

Truth

Prayers

Wednesday

Verse

Reflection

Truth

Prayers

Thursday

Verse

Reflection

Truth

Prayers

Inspiration

Friday

Verse

Reflection

Truth

Prayers

Saturday

Verse

Reflection

Truth

Prayers

Sunday

Verse

Reflection

Truth

Prayers

What encouraged you this week?

What can you do to encourage someone else?

Make it

Writing

- ☐
- ☐
- ☐
- ☐
- ☐
- ☐
- ☐

Marketing

- ☐
- ☐
- ☐
- ☐
- ☐
- ☐
- ☐

Craft

- ☐
- ☐
- ☐
- ☐
- ☐
- ☐
- ☐

Calls to Make

Errands

Happen

Project

- ☐
- ☐
- ☐
- ☐
- ☐
- ☐
- ☐

Other

- ☐
- ☐
- ☐
- ☐
- ☐
- ☐
- ☐

Menu

Monday
Tuesday
Wednesday
Thursday
Friday
Saturday
Sunday

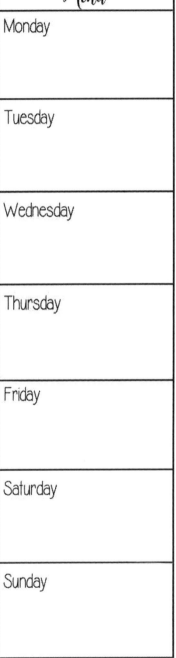

February

S	M	T	W	T	F	S
				1	2	3
4	5	6	7	8	9	10
11	12	13	14	15	16	17
18	19	20	21	22	23	24
25	26	27	28			

Do

Weekly Affirmation: _____

Monday	Tuesday	Wednesday
Dinner:	Dinner:	Dinner:
Exercise:	Exercise:	Exercise:

Notes

Water

	1	2	3	4	5	6	7	8
M								
T								
W								
T								
F								
S								
S								

It

	Thursday	Friday	Saturday

Dinner:

Exercise:

Dinner:

Exercise:

Sunday

Daily Habits	M	T	W	T	F	S	S

Appointments

Daily

Monday

Verse

Reflection

Truth

Prayers

Tuesday

Verse

Reflection

Truth

Prayers

Wednesday

Verse

Reflection

Truth

Prayers

Thursday

Verse

Reflection

Truth

Prayers

Inspiration

Friday

Verse

Reflection

Truth

Prayers

Saturday

Verse

Reflection

Truth

Prayers

Sunday

Verse

Reflection

Truth

Prayers

What encouraged you this week?

What can you do to encourage someone else?

Make it

Writing
- [ ]
- [ ]
- [ ]
- [ ]
- [ ]
- [ ]
- [ ]

Marketing
- [ ]
- [ ]
- [ ]
- [ ]
- [ ]
- [ ]
- [ ]

Craft
- [ ]
- [ ]
- [ ]
- [ ]
- [ ]
- [ ]
- [ ]

Calls to Make

Errands

Happen

Project

- [ ]
- [ ]
- [ ]
- [ ]
- [ ]
- [ ]
- [ ]

Other

- [ ]
- [ ]
- [ ]
- [ ]
- [ ]
- [ ]
- [ ]

Menu

Monday

Tuesday

Wednesday

Thursday

Friday

Saturday

Sunday

February

S	M	T	W	T	F	S
				1	2	3
4	5	6	7	8	9	10
11	12	13	14	15	16	17
18	19	20	21	22	23	24
25	26	27	28			

Do

Weekly Affirmation: _____

Monday	Tuesday	Wednesday
Dinner:	Dinner:	Dinner:
Exercise:	Exercise:	Exercise:

Notes

Water

	1	2	3	4	5	6	7	8
M								
T								
W								
T								
F								
S								
S								

It

Thursday	Friday	Saturday
		Sunday
Dinner:	Dinner:	
Exercise:	Exercise:	

Daily Habits	M	T	W	T	F	S	S

Appointments

Daily

Monday

Verse

Reflection

Truth

Prayers

Tuesday

Verse

Reflection

Truth

Prayers

Wednesday

Verse

Reflection

Truth

Prayers

Thursday

Verse

Reflection

Truth

Prayers

Inspiration

Friday

Verse

Reflection

Truth

Prayers

Saturday

Verse

Reflection

Truth

Prayers

Sunday

Verse

Reflection

Truth

Prayers

What encouraged you this week?

What can you do to encourage someone else?

Make it

Writing

- ☐
- ☐
- ☐
- ☐
- ☐
- ☐
- ☐

Marketing

- ☐
- ☐
- ☐
- ☐
- ☐
- ☐
- ☐

Craft

- ☐
- ☐
- ☐
- ☐
- ☐
- ☐
- ☐

Calls to Make

Errands

Happen

Project

- ☐
- ☐
- ☐
- ☐
- ☐
- ☐
- ☐

Other

- ☐
- ☐
- ☐
- ☐
- ☐
- ☐
- ☐

Menu

Monday

Tuesday

Wednesday

Thursday

Friday

Saturday

Sunday

February

S	M	T	W	T	F	S
				1	2	3
4	5	6	7	8	9	10
11	12	13	14	15	16	17
18	19	20	21	22	23	24
25	26	27	28			

Do

Weekly Affirmation: _____

Monday	Tuesday	Wednesday
Dinner:	Dinner:	Dinner:
Exercise:	Exercise:	Exercise:

Notes

Water

	1	2	3	4	5	6	7	8
M								
T								
W								
T								
F								
S								
S								

It

Thursday	Friday	Saturday

Dinner:

Dinner:

Exercise:

Exercise:

			Sunday

Daily Habits

	M	T	W	T	F	S	S

Appointments

Daily

Monday

Verse

Reflection

Truth

Prayers

Tuesday

Verse

Reflection

Truth

Prayers

Wednesday

Verse

Reflection

Truth

Prayers

Thursday

Verse

Reflection

Truth

Prayers

Inspiration

Friday

Verse

Reflection

Truth

Prayers

Saturday

Verse

Reflection

Truth

Prayers

Sunday

Verse

Reflection

Truth

Prayers

What encouraged you this week?

What can you do to encourage someone else?

Make it

Writing

☐
☐
☐
☐
☐
☐
☐

Marketing

☐
☐
☐
☐
☐
☐
☐

Craft

☐
☐
☐
☐
☐
☐
☐

Calls to Make

Errands

Happen

Project

- ☐
- ☐
- ☐
- ☐
- ☐
- ☐
- ☐

Other

- ☐
- ☐
- ☐
- ☐
- ☐
- ☐
- ☐

Menu

Monday	
Tuesday	
Wednesday	
Thursday	
Friday	
Saturday	
Sunday	

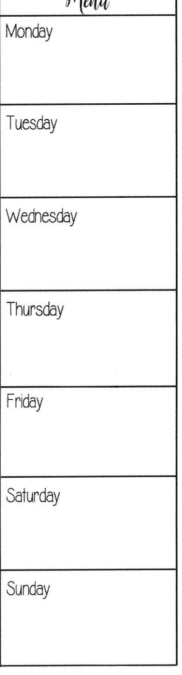

February

S	M	T	W	T	F	S
				1	2	3
4	5	6	7	8	9	10
11	12	13	14	15	16	17
18	19	20	21	22	23	24
25	26	27	28			

Do

Weekly Affirmation: _____

Monday	Tuesday	Wednesday
Dinner:	Dinner:	Dinner:
Exercise:	Exercise:	Exercise:

Notes

	1	2	3	4	5	6	7	8
M								
T								
W								
T								
F								
S								
S								

Water

It

Thursday	Friday	Saturday

		Sunday

Dinner:

Dinner:

Exercise:

Exercise:

Daily Habits	M	T	W	T	F	S	S

Appointments

Daily

Monday

Verse

Reflection

Truth

Prayers

Tuesday

Verse

Reflection

Truth

Prayers

Wednesday

Verse

Reflection

Truth

Prayers

Thursday

Verse

Reflection

Truth

Prayers

Inspiration

Friday

Verse

Reflection

Truth

Prayers

Saturday

Verse

Reflection

Truth

Prayers

Sunday

Verse

Reflection

Truth

Prayers

What encouraged you this week?

What can you do to encourage someone else?

Make it

Writing
- ☐
- ☐
- ☐
- ☐
- ☐
- ☐
- ☐

Marketing
- ☐
- ☐
- ☐
- ☐
- ☐
- ☐
- ☐

Craft
- ☐
- ☐
- ☐
- ☐
- ☐
- ☐
- ☐

Calls to Make

Errands

Happen

Project

- ☐
- ☐
- ☐
- ☐
- ☐
- ☐
- ☐

Other

- ☐
- ☐
- ☐
- ☐
- ☐
- ☐
- ☐

Menu

Monday
Tuesday
Wednesday
Thursday
Friday
Saturday
Sunday

February

S	M	T	W	T	F	S
				1	2	3
4	5	6	7	8	9	10
11	12	13	14	15	16	17
18	19	20	21	22	23	24
25	26	27	28			

Do

Weekly Affirmation: _____

Monday	Tuesday	Wednesday
Dinner:	Dinner:	Dinner:
Exercise:	Exercise:	Exercise:

Notes

Water

	1	2	3	4	5	6	7	8
M								
T								
W								
T								
F								
S								
S								

It

Thursday	Friday	Saturday
		Sunday
Dinner:	Dinner:	
Exercise:	Exercise:	

Daily Habits	M	T	W	T	F	S	S

Appointments

Monthly Review

Best

Accomplishments	Significant Events	What brought the most joy?

Worst

Biggest Challenges	Personal Struggles	Changes for Next Month

Truth:

How am I different?

Financial Tracker

Income	
Expenses	
Profit	
Tithe	
Savings	

Weight Tracker

	M	T	W	T	F
Week 1					
Week 2					
Week 3					
Week 4					
Week 5					

Books I Read

I am most proud of:

Ideas & inspiration for next month

A Month at a Glance

And now let us welcome the new year, full of things that never were.
Lydia Sweatt

Goals: Writing

Week 1: _____

Week 2: _____

Week 3: _____

Week 4: _____

Week 5: _____

Goals: Marketing

Week 1: _____

Week 2: _____

Week 3: _____

Week 4: _____

Week 5: _____

Goals: Craft

Week 1: _____

Week 2: _____

Week 3: _____

Week 4: _____

Week 5: _____

Goals: Other

Week 1: _____

Week 2: _____

Week 3: _____

Week 4: _____

Week 5: _____

Important Dates

_____

_____

_____

_____

_____

Things to Remember:

_____

_____

_____

_____

_____

I AM grateful FOR:

_____

_____

_____

_____

Favorite Writing Quote

March

Sunday	Monday	Tuesday	Wednesday
4	5	6	7
11	12	13	14
18	19	20	21
25	26	27	28

2018 ◇◆◇

Thursday	Friday	Saturday	Notes
1	2	3	
8	9	10	
15	16	17	
22	23	24	
29	30	31	

Daily

Monday

Verse

Reflection

Truth

Prayers

Tuesday

Verse

Reflection

Truth

Prayers

Wednesday

Verse

Reflection

Truth

Prayers

Thursday

Verse

Reflection

Truth

Prayers

Inspiration

Friday

Verse

Reflection

Truth

Prayers

Saturday

Verse

Reflection

Truth

Prayers

Sunday

Verse

Reflection

Truth

Prayers

What encouraged you this week?

What can you do to encourage someone else?

Make it

Writing
- ☐
- ☐
- ☐
- ☐
- ☐
- ☐
- ☐

Marketing
- ☐
- ☐
- ☐
- ☐
- ☐
- ☐
- ☐

Craft
- ☐
- ☐
- ☐
- ☐
- ☐
- ☐
- ☐

Calls to Make

Errands

Happen

Project

- [ ]
- [ ]
- [ ]
- [ ]
- [ ]
- [ ]
- [ ]

Other

- [ ]
- [ ]
- [ ]
- [ ]
- [ ]
- [ ]
- [ ]

Menu

Monday	
Tuesday	
Wednesday	
Thursday	
Friday	
Saturday	
Sunday	

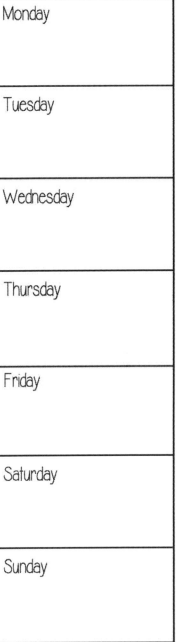

March

S	M	T	W	T	F	S
				1	2	3
4	5	6	7	8	9	10
11	12	13	14	15	16	17
18	19	20	21	22	23	24
25	26	27	28	29	30	31

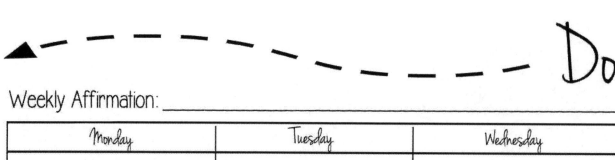

Weekly Affirmation: _____

Monday	Tuesday	Wednesday
Dinner:	Dinner:	Dinner:
Exercise:	Exercise:	Exercise:

Notes

Water

	1	2	3	4	5	6	7	8
M								
T								
W								
T								
F								
S								
S								

It

Thursday	Friday	Saturday

Sunday

Dinner:

Exercise:

Dinner:

Exercise:

Daily Habits

	M	T	W	T	F	S	S

Appointments

Daily

Monday

Verse

Reflection

Truth

Prayers

Tuesday

Verse

Reflection

Truth

Prayers

Wednesday

Verse

Reflection

Truth

Prayers

Thursday

Verse

Reflection

Truth

Prayers

Inspiration

Friday

Verse

Prayers

Reflection

Truth

Saturday

Verse

Prayers

Reflection

Truth

Sunday

Verse

Prayers

Reflection

Truth

What encouraged you this week?

What can you do to encourage someone else?

Make it

Writing

☐

☐

☐

☐

☐

☐

☐

Marketing

☐

☐

☐

☐

☐

☐

Craft

☐

☐

☐

☐

☐

☐

Calls to Make

Errands

Happen

Project

- ☐
- ☐
- ☐
- ☐
- ☐
- ☐
- ☐

Other

- ☐
- ☐
- ☐
- ☐
- ☐
- ☐
- ☐

Menu

Monday

Tuesday

Wednesday

Thursday

Friday

Saturday

Sunday

March

S	M	T	W	T	F	S
				1	2	3
4	5	6	7	8	9	10
11	12	13	14	15	16	17
18	19	20	21	22	23	24
25	26	27	28	29	30	31

Do

Weekly Affirmation: _____

Monday	Tuesday	Wednesday
Dinner:	Dinner:	Dinner:
Exercise:	Exercise:	Exercise:

Notes

Water

	1	2	3	4	5	6	7	8
M								
T								
W								
T								
F								
S								
S								

It ------>

Thursday	Friday	Saturday
		Sunday
Dinner:	Dinner:	
Exercise:	Exercise:	

Daily Habits

	M	T	W	T	F	S	S

Appointments

Daily

Monday

Verse

Reflection

Truth

Prayers

Tuesday

Verse

Reflection

Truth

Prayers

Wednesday

Verse

Reflection

Truth

Prayers

Thursday

Verse

Reflection

Truth

Prayers

Inspiration

Friday

Verse

Reflection

Truth

Prayers

Saturday

Verse

Reflection

Truth

Prayers

Sunday

Verse

Reflection

Truth

Prayers

What encouraged you this week?

What can you do to encourage someone else?

Make it

Writing

- ☐
- ☐
- ☐
- ☐
- ☐
- ☐
- ☐

Marketing

- ☐
- ☐
- ☐
- ☐
- ☐
- ☐
- ☐

Craft

- ☐
- ☐
- ☐
- ☐
- ☐
- ☐
- ☐

Calls to Make

Errands

Happen

Project

- ☐
- ☐
- ☐
- ☐
- ☐
- ☐
- ☐

Other

- ☐
- ☐
- ☐
- ☐
- ☐
- ☐
- ☐

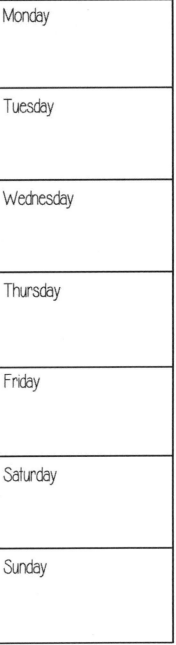

Menu

Monday

Tuesday

Wednesday

Thursday

Friday

Saturday

Sunday

March

S	M	T	W	T	F	S
				1	2	3
4	5	6	7	8	9	10
11	12	13	14	15	16	17
18	19	20	21	22	23	24
25	26	27	28	29	30	31

Do

Weekly Affirmation: _____

Monday	Tuesday	Wednesday

Dinner: Dinner: Dinner:

Exercise: Exercise: Exercise:

Notes

Water

	1	2	3	4	5	6	7	8
M								
T								
W								
T								
F								
S								
S								

It

Thursday	Friday	Saturday

Dinner:

Dinner:

Exercise:

Exercise:

Sunday

Daily Habits	M	T	W	T	F	S	S

Appointments

Daily

Monday
Verse

Reflection

Truth

Prayers

Tuesday
Verse

Reflection

Truth

Prayers

Wednesday
Verse

Reflection

Truth

Prayers

Thursday
Verse

Reflection

Truth

Prayers

Inspiration

Friday

Verse

Reflection

Truth

Prayers

Saturday

Verse

Reflection

Truth

Prayers

Sunday

Verse

Reflection

Truth

Prayers

What encouraged you this week?

What can you do to encourage someone else?

Make it

Writing

☐

☐

☐

☐

☐

☐

☐

Marketing

☐

☐

☐

☐

☐

☐

☐

Craft

☐

☐

☐

☐

☐

☐

☐

Calls to Make

Errands

Happen

Project

- ☐
- ☐
- ☐
- ☐
- ☐
- ☐
- ☐

Other

- ☐
- ☐
- ☐
- ☐
- ☐
- ☐
- ☐

Menu

Monday
Tuesday
Wednesday
Thursday
Friday
Saturday
Sunday

March

S	M	T	W	T	F	S
				1	2	3
4	5	6	7	8	9	10
11	12	13	14	15	16	17
18	19	20	21	22	23	24
25	26	27	28	29	30	31

Do

Weekly Affirmation: _____

Monday	Tuesday	Wednesday
Dinner:	Dinner:	Dinner:
Exercise:	Exercise:	Exercise:

Notes

Water

	1	2	3	4	5	6	7	8
M								
T								
W								
T								
F								
S								
S								

It - - - - - - - - - - - - - - ▶

Thursday	Friday	Saturday
		Sunday
Dinner:	Dinner:	
Exercise:	Exercise:	

Daily Habits	M	T	W	T	F	S	S

Appointments

Daily

Monday
Verse

Reflection

Truth

Prayers

Tuesday
Verse

Reflection

Truth

Prayers

Wednesday
Verse

Reflection

Truth

Prayers

Thursday
Verse

Reflection

Truth

Prayers

Inspiration

Friday

Verse

Reflection

Truth

Prayers

Saturday

Verse

Reflection

Truth

Prayers

Sunday

Verse

Reflection

Truth

Prayers

What encouraged you this week?

What can you do to encourage someone else?

Make it

Writing

- ☐
- ☐
- ☐
- ☐
- ☐
- ☐
- ☐

Marketing

- ☐
- ☐
- ☐
- ☐
- ☐
- ☐
- ☐

Craft

- ☐
- ☐
- ☐
- ☐
- ☐
- ☐
- ☐

Calls to Make

Errands

Happen

Project

- ☐
- ☐
- ☐
- ☐
- ☐
- ☐
- ☐

Other

- ☐
- ☐
- ☐
- ☐
- ☐
- ☐

Menu

Monday
Tuesday
Wednesday
Thursday
Friday
Saturday
Sunday

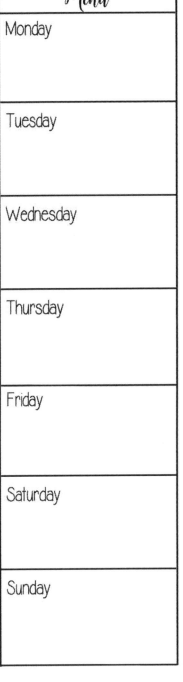

March

S	M	T	W	T	F	S
				1	2	3
4	5	6	7	8	9	10
11	12	13	14	15	16	17
18	19	20	21	22	23	24
25	26	27	28	29	30	31

Do

Weekly Affirmation: _____

Monday	Tuesday	Wednesday
Dinner:	Dinner:	Dinner:
Exercise:	Exercise:	Exercise:

Notes

Water

	1	2	3	4	5	6	7	8
M								
T								
W								
T								
F								
S								
S								

It ----------➤

Thursday	Friday	Saturday
Dinner:	Dinner:	

Sunday

Daily Habits	M	T	W	T	F	S	S

Appointments

Monthly Review

→ Best ←

Accomplishments	Significant Events	What brought the most joy?

← Worst →

Biggest Challenges	Personal Struggles	Changes for Next Month

Truth:

How am I different?

Financial Tracker

Income	
Expenses	
Profit	
Tithe	
Savings	

Weight Tracker

	M	T	W	T	F
Week 1					
Week 2					
Week 3					
Week 4					
Week 5					

Books I Read

I am most proud of:

Ideas & inspiration for next month

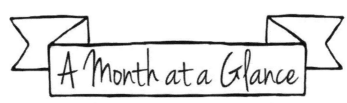

A Month at a Glance

And now let us welcome the new year, full of things that never were.
Lydia Sweatt

Goals: Writing

Week 1: _____

Week 2: _____

Week 3: _____

Week 4: _____

Week 5: _____

Goals: Marketing

Week 1: _____

Week 2: _____

Week 3: _____

Week 4: _____

Week 5: _____

Goals: Craft

Week 1: _____

Week 2: _____

Week 3: _____

Week 4: _____

Week 5: _____

Goals: Other

Week 1: _____

Week 2: _____

Week 3: _____

Week 4: _____

Week 5: _____

Important Dates

_____

_____

_____

_____

Things to Remember:

_____

_____

_____

_____

I AM grateful FOR:

_____

_____

_____

_____

Favorite Writing Quote

April

Sunday	Monday	Tuesday	Wednesday
1	2	3	4
8	9	10	11
15	16	17	18
22	23	24	25
29	30		

2018 ◇◆◇

Thursday	Friday	Saturday	Notes
5	6	7	
12	13	14	
19	20	21	
26	27	28	

Daily

Monday

Verse

Reflection

Truth

Prayers

Tuesday

Verse

Reflection

Truth

Prayers

Wednesday

Verse

Reflection

Truth

Prayers

Thursday

Verse

Reflection

Truth

Prayers

Inspiration

Friday

Verse

Reflection

Truth

Prayers

Saturday

Verse

Reflection

Truth

Prayers

Sunday

Verse

Reflection

Truth

Prayers

What encouraged you this week?

What can you do to encourage someone else?

Make it

Writing

- ☐
- ☐
- ☐
- ☐
- ☐
- ☐
- ☐

Marketing

- ☐
- ☐
- ☐
- ☐
- ☐
- ☐
- ☐

Craft

- ☐
- ☐
- ☐
- ☐
- ☐
- ☐
- ☐

Calls to Make

Errands

Happen

Project

- [ ]
- [ ]
- [ ]
- [ ]
- [ ]
- [ ]
- [ ]

Other

- [ ]
- [ ]
- [ ]
- [ ]
- [ ]
- [ ]
- [ ]

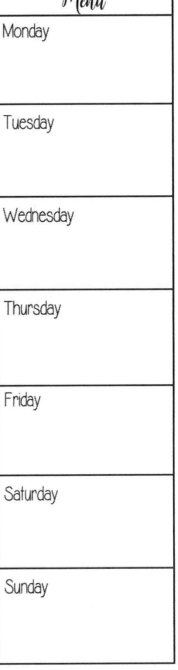

Menu

Monday
Tuesday
Wednesday
Thursday
Friday
Saturday
Sunday

April

S	M	T	W	T	F	S
1	2	3	4	5	6	7
8	9	10	11	12	13	14
15	16	17	18	19	20	21
22	23	24	25	26	27	28
29	30					

Do

Weekly Affirmation: _____

Monday	Tuesday	Wednesday
Dinner:	Dinner:	Dinner:
Exercise:	Exercise:	Exercise:

Notes

Water

	1	2	3	4	5	6	7	8
M								
T								
W								
T								
F								
S								
S								

It

Thursday	Friday	Saturday

	Sunday

Dinner:

Dinner:

Exercise:

Exercise:

Daily Habits	M	T	W	T	F	S	S

Appointments

Daily

Monday

Verse

Reflection

Truth

Prayers

Tuesday

Verse

Reflection

Truth

Prayers

Wednesday

Verse

Reflection

Truth

Prayers

Thursday

Verse

Reflection

Truth

Prayers

Inspiration

Friday

Verse

Reflection

Truth

Prayers

Saturday

Verse

Reflection

Truth

Prayers

Sunday

Verse

Reflection

Truth

Prayers

What encouraged you this week?

What can you do to encourage someone else?

Make it

Writing

☐

☐

☐

☐

☐

☐

☐

Marketing

☐

☐

☐

☐

☐

☐

☐

Craft

☐

☐

☐

☐

☐

☐

☐

Calls to Make

Errands

Happen →

Project

- ☐
- ☐
- ☐
- ☐
- ☐
- ☐
- ☐

Other

- ☐
- ☐
- ☐
- ☐
- ☐
- ☐
- ☐

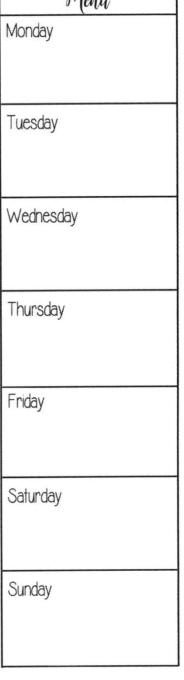

Menu

Monday
Tuesday
Wednesday
Thursday
Friday
Saturday
Sunday

April

S	M	T	W	T	F	S
1	2	3	4	5	6	7
8	9	10	11	12	13	14
15	16	17	18	19	20	21
22	23	24	25	26	27	28
29	30					

Do

Weekly Affirmation: _____

Monday	Tuesday	Wednesday
Dinner:	Dinner:	Dinner:
Exercise:	Exercise:	Exercise:

Notes

Water

	1	2	3	4	5	6	7	8
M								
T								
W								
T								
F								
S								
S								

It ------- ▶

Thursday	Friday	Saturday
		Sunday
Dinner:	Dinner:	
Exercise:	Exercise:	

Daily Habits

	M	T	W	T	F	S	S

Appointments

Daily

Monday

Verse

Reflection

Truth

Prayers

Tuesday

Verse

Reflection

Truth

Prayers

Wednesday

Verse

Reflection

Truth

Prayers

Thursday

Verse

Reflection

Truth

Prayers

Inspiration

Friday

Verse

Reflection

Truth

Prayers

Saturday

Verse

Reflection

Truth

Prayers

Sunday

Verse

Reflection

Truth

Prayers

What encouraged you this week?

What can you do to encourage someone else?

Make it

Writing

- ☐
- ☐
- ☐
- ☐
- ☐
- ☐
- ☐

Marketing

- ☐
- ☐
- ☐
- ☐
- ☐
- ☐
- ☐

Craft

- ☐
- ☐
- ☐
- ☐
- ☐
- ☐
- ☐

Calls to Make

Errands

Happen

Project

- ☐
- ☐
- ☐
- ☐
- ☐
- ☐
- ☐

Other

- ☐
- ☐
- ☐
- ☐
- ☐
- ☐
- ☐

Menu

Monday

Tuesday

Wednesday

Thursday

Friday

Saturday

Sunday

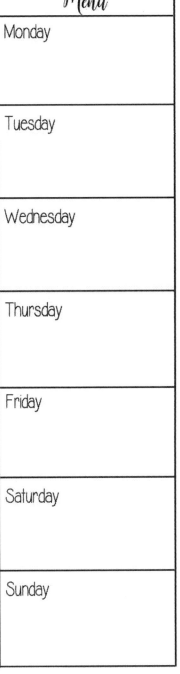

April

S	M	T	W	T	F	S
1	2	3	4	5	6	7
8	9	10	11	12	13	14
15	16	17	18	19	20	21
22	23	24	25	26	27	28
29	30					

Do

Weekly Affirmation: _____

Monday	Tuesday	Wednesday
Dinner:	Dinner:	Dinner:
Exercise:	Exercise:	Exercise:

Notes

Water	1	2	3	4	5	6	7	8
M								
T								
W								
T								
F								
S								
S								

It

Thursday	Friday	Saturday
Dinner:	Dinner:	Sunday
Exercise:	Exercise:	

Daily Habits

	M	T	W	T	F	S	S

Appointments

Daily

Monday

Verse

Reflection

Truth

Prayers

Tuesday

Verse

Reflection

Truth

Prayers

Wednesday

Verse

Reflection

Truth

Prayers

Thursday

Verse

Reflection

Truth

Prayers

Inspiration

Friday

Verse

Reflection

Truth

Prayers

Saturday

Verse

Reflection

Truth

Prayers

Sunday

Verse

Reflection

Truth

Prayers

What encouraged you this week?

What can you do to encourage someone else?

Make it

←

Writing

☐

☐

☐

☐

☐

☐

☐

Marketing

☐

☐

☐

☐

☐

☐

☐

Craft

☐

☐

☐

☐

☐

☐

☐

Calls to Make

Errands

Happen

Project

- ☐
- ☐
- ☐
- ☐
- ☐
- ☐
- ☐

Other

- ☐
- ☐
- ☐
- ☐
- ☐
- ☐
- ☐

Menu

Monday
Tuesday
Wednesday
Thursday
Friday
Saturday
Sunday

April

S	M	T	W	T	F	S
1	2	3	4	5	6	7
8	9	10	11	12	13	14
15	16	17	18	19	20	21
22	23	24	25	26	27	28
29	30					

Do

Weekly Affirmation: _____

Monday	Tuesday	Wednesday
Dinner:	Dinner:	Dinner:
Exercise:	Exercise:	Exercise:

Notes

Water

	1	2	3	4	5	6	7	8
M								
T								
W								
T								
F								
S								
S								

It

Thursday	Friday	Saturday
Dinner:	Dinner:	Sunday
Exercise:	Exercise:	

Daily Habits

	M	T	W	T	F	S	S

Appointments

Daily

Monday

Verse

Reflection

Truth

Prayers

Tuesday

Verse

Reflection

Truth

Prayers

Wednesday

Verse

Reflection

Truth

Prayers

Thursday

Verse

Reflection

Truth

Prayers

Inspiration

Friday

Verse

Reflection

Truth

Prayers

Saturday

Verse

Reflection

Truth

Prayers

Sunday

Verse

Reflection

Truth

Prayers

What encouraged you this week?

What can you do to encourage someone else?

Make it

Writing	Marketing	Craft
☐	☐	☐
☐	☐	☐
☐	☐	☐
☐	☐	☐
☐	☐	☐
☐	☐	☐
☐	☐	☐

Calls to Make

Errands

Happen

Project

- [ ]
- [ ]
- [ ]
- [ ]
- [ ]
- [ ]
- [ ]

Other

- [ ]
- [ ]
- [ ]
- [ ]
- [ ]
- [ ]
- [ ]

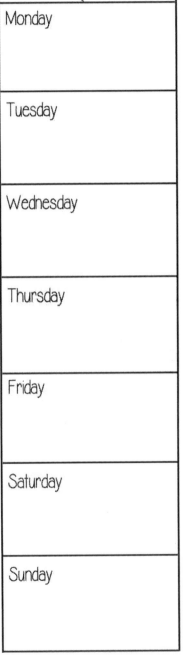

Menu

Monday

Tuesday

Wednesday

Thursday

Friday

Saturday

Sunday

April

S	M	T	W	T	F	S
1	2	3	4	5	6	7
8	9	10	11	12	13	14
15	16	17	18	19	20	21
22	23	24	25	26	27	28
29	30					

Do

Weekly Affirmation: _____

Monday	Tuesday	Wednesday
Dinner:	Dinner:	Dinner:
Exercise:	Exercise:	Exercise:

Notes

Water

	1	2	3	4	5	6	7	8
M								
T								
W								
T								
F								
S								
S								

It

	Thursday	Friday	Saturday

Sunday

Dinner:

Dinner:

Exercise:

Exercise:

Daily Habits	M	T	W	T	F	S	S

Appointments

Monthly Review

← **Best** →

Accomplishments	Significant Events	What brought the most joy?

← **Worst** →

Biggest Challenges	Personal Struggles	Changes for Next Month

Truth:

How am I different?

Financial Tracker

Income	
Expenses	
Profit	
Tithe	
Savings	

Weight Tracker

	M	T	W	T	F
Week 1					
Week 2					
Week 3					
Week 4					
Week 5					

Books I Read

I am most proud of:

Ideas & inspiration for next month

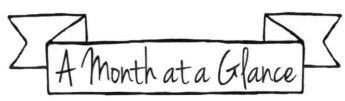

A Month at a Glance

And now let us welcome the new year, full of things that never were.
Lydia Sweatt

Goals: Writing

Week 1: _____
Week 2: _____
Week 3: _____
Week 4: _____
Week 5: _____

Goals: Marketing

Week 1: _____
Week 2: _____
Week 3: _____
Week 4: _____
Week 5: _____

Goals: Craft

Week 1: _____
Week 2: _____
Week 3: _____
Week 4: _____
Week 5: _____

Goals: Other

Week 1: _____
Week 2: _____
Week 3: _____
Week 4: _____
Week 5: _____

Important Dates

_____
_____
_____
_____

Things to Remember:

_____
_____
_____
_____
_____

I AM grateful FOR:

_____
_____
_____

Favorite Writing Quote

May

Sunday	Monday	Tuesday	Wednesday
		1	2
6	7	8	9
13	14	15	16
20	21	22	23
27	28	29	30

2018 ◇◈◇

Thursday	Friday	Saturday	Notes
3	4	5	
10	11	12	
17	18	19	
24	25	26	
31			

Daily

Monday

Verse

Prayers

Reflection

Truth

Tuesday

Verse

Prayers

Reflection

Truth

Wednesday

Verse

Prayers

Reflection

Truth

Thursday

Verse

Prayers

Reflection

Truth

Inspiration

Friday

Verse

Reflection

Truth

Prayers

Saturday

Verse

Reflection

Truth

Prayers

Sunday

Verse

Reflection

Truth

Prayers

What encouraged you this week?

What can you do to encourage someone else?

Make it

Writing

- ☐
- ☐
- ☐
- ☐
- ☐
- ☐
- ☐

Marketing

- ☐
- ☐
- ☐
- ☐
- ☐
- ☐
- ☐

Craft

- ☐
- ☐
- ☐
- ☐
- ☐
- ☐
- ☐

Calls to Make

Errands

Happen

Project

- ☐
- ☐
- ☐
- ☐
- ☐
- ☐
- ☐

Other

- ☐
- ☐
- ☐
- ☐
- ☐
- ☐

Menu

Monday
Tuesday
Wednesday
Thursday
Friday
Saturday
Sunday

May

S	M	T	W	T	F	S
		1	2	3	4	5
6	7	8	9	10	11	12
13	14	15	16	17	18	19
20	21	22	23	24	25	26
27	28	29	30	31		

Do

Weekly Affirmation: _____

Monday	Tuesday	Wednesday
Dinner:	Dinner:	Dinner:
Exercise:	Exercise:	Exercise:

Notes

Water

	1	2	3	4	5	6	7	8
M								
T								
W								
T								
F								
S								
S								

It

Thursday	Friday	Saturday

Sunday

Dinner:

Dinner:

Exercise:

Exercise:

Daily Habits	M	T	W	T	F	S	S

Appointments

Daily

Monday

Verse

Reflection

Truth

Prayers

Tuesday

Verse

Reflection

Truth

Prayers

Wednesday

Verse

Reflection

Truth

Prayers

Thursday

Verse

Reflection

Truth

Prayers

Inspiration

Friday

Verse

Prayers

Reflection

Truth

Saturday

Verse

Prayers

Reflection

Truth

Sunday

Verse

Prayers

Reflection

Truth

What encouraged you this week?

What can you do to encourage someone else?

 Make it

Writing
- ☐
- ☐
- ☐
- ☐
- ☐
- ☐
- ☐

Marketing
- ☐
- ☐
- ☐
- ☐
- ☐
- ☐
- ☐

Craft
- ☐
- ☐
- ☐
- ☐
- ☐
- ☐
- ☐

Calls to Make

Errands

Happen

Project

- ☐
- ☐
- ☐
- ☐
- ☐
- ☐
- ☐

Other

- ☐
- ☐
- ☐
- ☐
- ☐
- ☐

Menu

Monday	
Tuesday	
Wednesday	
Thursday	
Friday	
Saturday	
Sunday	

May

S	M	T	W	T	F	S
		1	2	3	4	5
6	7	8	9	10	11	12
13	14	15	16	17	18	19
20	21	22	23	24	25	26
27	28	29	30	31		

Do

Weekly Affirmation: _____

Monday	Tuesday	Wednesday
Dinner:	Dinner:	Dinner:
Exercise:	Exercise:	Exercise:

Notes

Water

	1	2	3	4	5	6	7	8
M								
T								
W								
T								
F								
S								
S								

It

Thursday	Friday	Saturday

		Sunday

Dinner:

Dinner:

Exercise:

Exercise:

Daily Habits	M	T	W	T	F	S	S

Appointments

Daily

Monday

Verse

Reflection

Truth

Prayers

Tuesday

Verse

Reflection

Truth

Prayers

Wednesday

Verse

Reflection

Truth

Prayers

Thursday

Verse

Reflection

Truth

Prayers

Inspiration

Friday

Verse

Prayers

Reflection

Truth

Saturday

Verse

Prayers

Reflection

Truth

Sunday

Verse

Prayers

Reflection

Truth

What encouraged you this week?

What can you do to encourage someone else?

Make it

Writing

☐
☐
☐
☐
☐
☐
☐

Marketing

☐
☐
☐
☐
☐
☐
☐

Craft

☐
☐
☐
☐
☐
☐
☐

Calls to Make

Errands

Happen

Project

- ☐
- ☐
- ☐
- ☐
- ☐
- ☐
- ☐

Other

- ☐
- ☐
- ☐
- ☐
- ☐
- ☐
- ☐

Menu

| Monday |
| Tuesday |
| Wednesday |
| Thursday |
| Friday |
| Saturday |
| Sunday |

May

S	M	T	W	T	F	S
		1	2	3	4	5
6	7	8	9	10	11	12
13	14	15	16	17	18	19
20	21	22	23	24	25	26
27	28	29	30	31		

Do

Weekly Affirmation: _____

Monday	Tuesday	Wednesday
Dinner:	Dinner:	Dinner:
Exercise:	Exercise:	Exercise:

Notes

Water

	1	2	3	4	5	6	7	8
M								
T								
W								
T								
F								
S								
S								

It

Thursday	Friday	Saturday
		Sunday
Dinner:	Dinner:	
Exercise:	Exercise:	

Daily Habits

	M	T	W	T	F	S	S

Appointments

Daily

Monday

Verse

Reflection

Truth

Prayers

Tuesday

Verse

Reflection

Truth

Prayers

Wednesday

Verse

Reflection

Truth

Prayers

Thursday

Verse

Reflection

Truth

Prayers

Inspiration

Friday

Verse

Reflection

Truth

Prayers

Saturday

Verse

Reflection

Truth

Prayers

Sunday

Verse

Reflection

Truth

Prayers

What encouraged you this week?

What can you do to encourage someone else?

Make it

Writing

- [ ]
- [ ]
- [ ]
- [ ]
- [ ]
- [ ]
- [ ]

Marketing

- [ ]
- [ ]
- [ ]
- [ ]
- [ ]
- [ ]
- [ ]

Craft

- [ ]
- [ ]
- [ ]
- [ ]
- [ ]
- [ ]

Calls to Make

Errands

Happen ⟶

Project
- ☐
- ☐
- ☐
- ☐
- ☐
- ☐
- ☐

Other
- ☐
- ☐
- ☐
- ☐
- ☐
- ☐

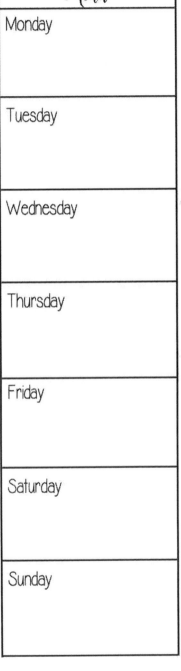

Menu

Monday	
Tuesday	
Wednesday	
Thursday	
Friday	
Saturday	
Sunday	

May

S	M	T	W	T	F	S
		1	2	3	4	5
6	7	8	9	10	11	12
13	14	15	16	17	18	19
20	21	22	23	24	25	26
27	28	29	30	31		

Do

Weekly Affirmation: _____

Monday	Tuesday	Wednesday
Dinner:	Dinner:	Dinner:
Exercise:	Exercise:	Exercise:

Notes

Water

	1	2	3	4	5	6	7	8
M								
T								
W								
T								
F								
S								
S								

It

Thursday	Friday	Saturday
		Sunday
Dinner:	Dinner:	
Exercise:	Exercise:	

Daily Habits

	M	T	W	T	F	S	S

Appointments

Daily

Monday
Verse

Reflection

Truth

Prayers

Tuesday
Verse

Reflection

Truth

Prayers

Wednesday
Verse

Reflection

Truth

Prayers

Thursday
Verse

Reflection

Truth

Prayers

Inspiration

Friday

Verse

Prayers

Reflection

Truth

Saturday

Verse

Prayers

Reflection

Truth

Sunday

Verse

Prayers

Reflection

Truth

What encouraged you this week?

What can you do to encourage someone else?

Make it

Writing

☐
☐
☐
☐
☐
☐
☐

Marketing

☐
☐
☐
☐
☐
☐
☐

Craft

☐
☐
☐
☐
☐
☐
☐

Calls to Make

Errands

Happen

Project

- [ ]
- [ ]
- [ ]
- [ ]
- [ ]
- [ ]
- [ ]

Other

- [ ]
- [ ]
- [ ]
- [ ]
- [ ]
- [ ]
- [ ]

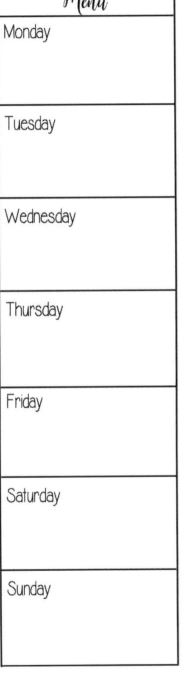

Menu

Monday

Tuesday

Wednesday

Thursday

Friday

Saturday

Sunday

May

S	M	T	W	T	F	S
		1	2	3	4	5
6	7	8	9	10	11	12
13	14	15	16	17	18	19
20	21	22	23	24	25	26
27	28	29	30	31		

Do

Weekly Affirmation: _____

Monday	Tuesday	Wednesday
Dinner:	Dinner:	Dinner:
Exercise:	Exercise:	Exercise:

Notes

	1	2	3	4	5	6	7	8
M								
T								
W								
T								
F								
S								
S								

Water

It ------➤

Thursday	Friday	Saturday
		Sunday
Dinner:	Dinner:	
Exercise:	Exercise:	

Daily Habits

	M	T	W	T	F	S	S

Appointments

Monthly Review

→ **Best** ←

Accomplishments	Significant Events	What brought the most joy?

← **Worst** →

Biggest Challenges	Personal Struggles	Changes for Next Month

Truth:

How am I different?

Financial Tracker

Income	
Expenses	
Profit	
Tithe	
Savings	

Weight Tracker

	M	T	W	T	F
Week 1					
Week 2					
Week 3					
Week 4					
Week 5					

Books I Read

I am most proud of:

Ideas & inspiration for next month

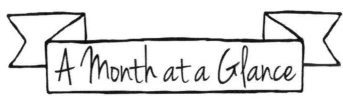

A Month at a Glance

And now let us welcome the new year, full of things that never were.
Lydia Sweatt

Goals: Writing

Week 1: _____

Week 2: _____

Week 3: _____

Week 4: _____

Week 5: _____

Goals: Marketing

Week 1: _____

Week 2: _____

Week 3: _____

Week 4: _____

Week 5: _____

Goals: Craft

Week 1: _____

Week 2: _____

Week 3: _____

Week 4: _____

Week 5: _____

Goals: Other

Week 1: _____

Week 2: _____

Week 3: _____

Week 4: _____

Week 5: _____

Important Dates

_____

_____

_____

_____

_____

Things to Remember:

_____

_____

_____

_____

_____

I AM grateful FOR:

_____

_____

_____

_____

Favorite Writing Quote

June

Sunday	Monday	Tuesday	Wednesday
3	4	5	6
10	11	12	13
17	18	19	20
24	25	26	27

2018 ◇◈◇

Thursday	Friday	Saturday	Notes
	1	2	
7	8	9	
14	15	16	
21	22	23	
28	29	30	

Daily

Monday

Verse

Prayers

Reflection

Truth

Tuesday

Verse

Prayers

Reflection

Truth

Wednesday

Verse

Prayers

Reflection

Truth

Thursday

Verse

Prayers

Reflection

Truth

Inspiration

Friday

Verse

Reflection

Truth

Prayers

Saturday

Verse

Reflection

Truth

Prayers

Sunday

Verse

Reflection

Truth

Prayers

What encouraged you this week?

What can you do to encourage someone else?

Make it

Writing

- ☐
- ☐
- ☐
- ☐
- ☐
- ☐
- ☐

Marketing

- ☐
- ☐
- ☐
- ☐
- ☐
- ☐
- ☐

Craft

- ☐
- ☐
- ☐
- ☐
- ☐
- ☐
- ☐

Calls to Make

Errands

Happen

Project

- ☐
- ☐
- ☐
- ☐
- ☐
- ☐
- ☐

Other

- ☐
- ☐
- ☐
- ☐
- ☐
- ☐
- ☐

Menu

Monday

Tuesday

Wednesday

Thursday

Friday

Saturday

Sunday

June

S	M	T	W	T	F	S
					1	2
3	4	5	6	7	8	9
10	11	12	13	14	15	16
17	18	19	20	21	22	23
24	25	26	27	28	29	30

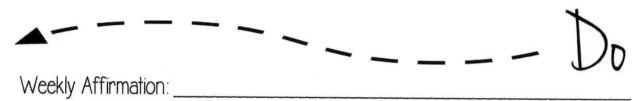

Weekly Affirmation: _____

Monday	Tuesday	Wednesday
Dinner:	Dinner:	Dinner:
Exercise:	Exercise:	Exercise:

Notes

Water

	1	2	3	4	5	6	7	8
M								
T								
W								
T								
F								
S								
S								

It

Thursday	Friday	Saturday
Dinner:	Dinner:	**Sunday**
Exercise:	Exercise:	

Daily Habits	M	T	W	T	F	S	S

Appointments

Daily

Monday

Verse

Reflection

Truth

Prayers

Tuesday

Verse

Reflection

Truth

Prayers

Wednesday

Verse

Reflection

Truth

Prayers

Thursday

Verse

Reflection

Truth

Prayers

Inspiration

Friday

Verse

Prayers

Reflection

Truth

Saturday

Verse

Prayers

Reflection

Truth

Sunday

Verse

Prayers

Reflection

Truth

What encouraged you this week?

What can you do to encourage someone else?

Make it

Writing

☐

☐

☐

☐

☐

☐

☐

Marketing

☐

☐

☐

☐

☐

☐

☐

Craft

☐

☐

☐

☐

☐

☐

☐

Calls to Make

Errands

Happen

Project

- ☐
- ☐
- ☐
- ☐
- ☐
- ☐
- ☐

Other

- ☐
- ☐
- ☐
- ☐
- ☐
- ☐
- ☐

Menu

Day	
Monday	
Tuesday	
Wednesday	
Thursday	
Friday	
Saturday	
Sunday	

June

S	M	T	W	T	F	S
					1	2
3	4	5	6	7	8	9
10	11	12	13	14	15	16
17	18	19	20	21	22	23
24	25	26	27	28	29	30

Do

Weekly Affirmation: _____

Monday	Tuesday	Wednesday
Dinner:	Dinner:	Dinner:
Exercise:	Exercise:	Exercise:

Notes

Water

	1	2	3	4	5	6	7	8
M								
T								
W								
T								
F								
S								
S								

It

Thursday	Friday	Saturday

Sunday

Dinner:

Dinner:

Exercise:

Exercise:

Daily Habits	M	T	W	T	F	S	S

Appointments

Daily

Monday

Verse

Reflection

Truth

Prayers

Tuesday

Verse

Reflection

Truth

Prayers

Wednesday

Verse

Reflection

Truth

Prayers

Thursday

Verse

Reflection

Truth

Prayers

Inspiration

Friday

Verse

Reflection

Truth

Prayers

Saturday

Verse

Reflection

Truth

Prayers

Sunday

Verse

Reflection

Truth

Prayers

What encouraged you this week?

What can you do to encourage someone else?

Make it

Writing
- [ ]
- [ ]
- [ ]
- [ ]
- [ ]
- [ ]
- [ ]

Marketing
- [ ]
- [ ]
- [ ]
- [ ]
- [ ]
- [ ]
- [ ]

Craft
- [ ]
- [ ]
- [ ]
- [ ]
- [ ]
- [ ]
- [ ]

Calls to Make

Errands

Happen

Project

- [ ]
- [ ]
- [ ]
- [ ]
- [ ]
- [ ]
- [ ]

Other

- [ ]
- [ ]
- [ ]
- [ ]
- [ ]
- [ ]

Menu

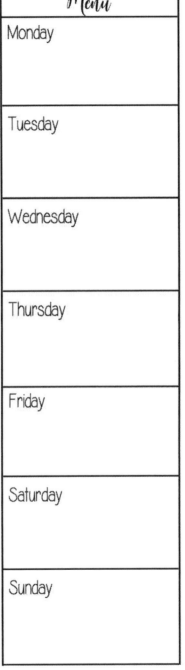

Monday

Tuesday

Wednesday

Thursday

Friday

Saturday

Sunday

June

S	M	T	W	T	F	S
					1	2
3	4	5	6	7	8	9
10	11	12	13	14	15	16
17	18	19	20	21	22	23
24	25	26	27	28	29	30

Do

Weekly Affirmation: _____

Monday	Tuesday	Wednesday
Dinner:	Dinner:	Dinner:
Exercise:	Exercise:	Exercise:

Notes

Water

	1	2	3	4	5	6	7	8
M								
T								
W								
T								
F								
S								
S								

It

Thursday	Friday	Saturday
		Sunday
Dinner:	Dinner:	
Exercise:	Exercise:	

Daily Habits

	M	T	W	T	F	S	S

Appointments

Daily

Monday

Verse

Reflection

Truth

Prayers

Tuesday

Verse

Reflection

Truth

Prayers

Wednesday

Verse

Reflection

Truth

Prayers

Thursday

Verse

Reflection

Truth

Prayers

Inspiration

Friday

Verse

Reflection

Truth

Prayers

Saturday

Verse

Reflection

Truth

Prayers

Sunday

Verse

Reflection

Truth

Prayers

What encouraged you this week?

What can you do to encourage someone else?

Make it

Writing

- [ ]
- [ ]
- [ ]
- [ ]
- [ ]
- [ ]
- [ ]

Marketing

- [ ]
- [ ]
- [ ]
- [ ]
- [ ]
- [ ]
- [ ]

Craft

- [ ]
- [ ]
- [ ]
- [ ]
- [ ]
- [ ]
- [ ]

Calls to Make

Errands

Happen

Project

- ☐
- ☐
- ☐
- ☐
- ☐
- ☐
- ☐

Other

- ☐
- ☐
- ☐
- ☐
- ☐
- ☐
- ☐

Menu

Monday
Tuesday
Wednesday
Thursday
Friday
Saturday
Sunday

June

S	M	T	W	T	F	S
					1	2
3	4	5	6	7	8	9
10	11	12	13	14	15	16
17	18	19	20	21	22	23
24	25	26	27	28	29	30

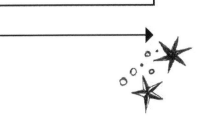

Weekly Affirmation: _____

Monday	Tuesday	Wednesday
Dinner:	Dinner:	Dinner:
Exercise:	Exercise:	Exercise:

Notes

Water

	1	2	3	4	5	6	7	8
M								
T								
W								
T								
F								
S								
S								

It ------>

Thursday	Friday	Saturday
		Sunday
Dinner:	Dinner:	
Exercise:	Exercise:	

Daily Habits

	M	T	W	T	F	S	S

Appointments

Daily

Monday

Verse

Reflection

Truth

Prayers

Tuesday

Verse

Reflection

Truth

Prayers

Wednesday

Verse

Reflection

Truth

Prayers

Thursday

Verse

Reflection

Truth

Prayers

Inspiration

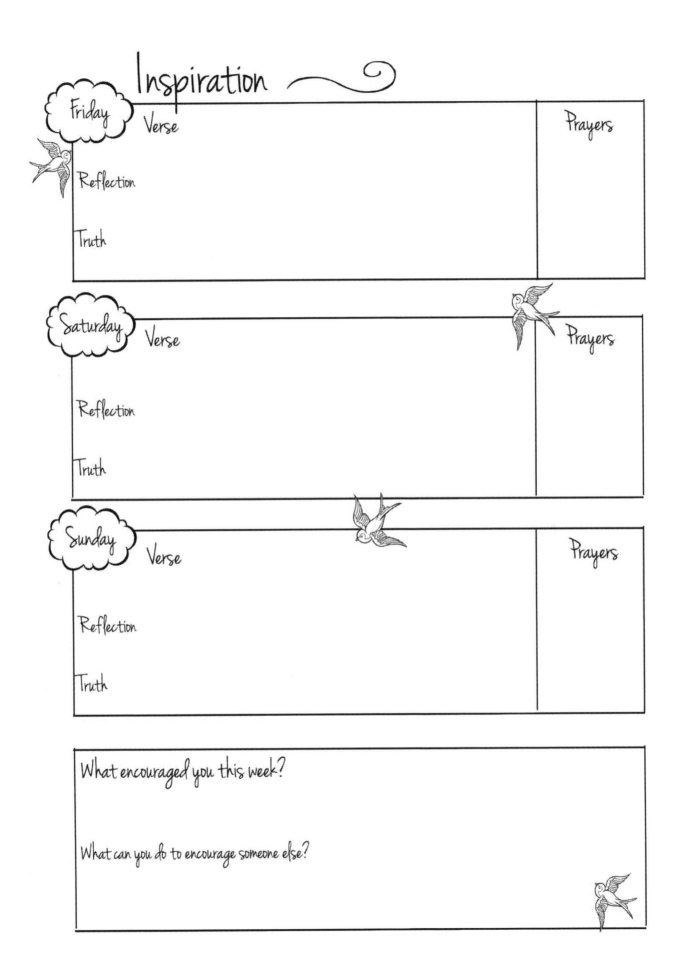

Friday

Verse

Reflection

Truth

Prayers

Saturday

Verse

Reflection

Truth

Prayers

Sunday

Verse

Reflection

Truth

Prayers

What encouraged you this week?

What can you do to encourage someone else?

Make it

Writing

☐

☐

☐

☐

☐

☐

☐

Marketing

☐

☐

☐

☐

☐

☐

☐

Craft

☐

☐

☐

☐

☐

☐

☐

Calls to Make

Errands

Happen

Project

- ☐
- ☐
- ☐
- ☐
- ☐
- ☐
- ☐

Other

- ☐
- ☐
- ☐
- ☐
- ☐
- ☐
- ☐

Menu

Monday

Tuesday

Wednesday

Thursday

Friday

Saturday

Sunday

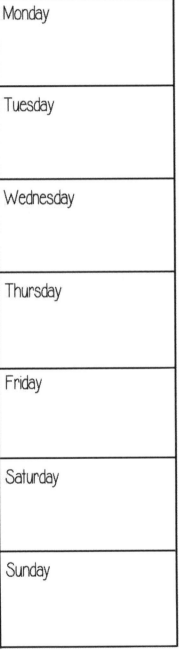

June

S	M	T	W	T	F	S
					1	2
3	4	5	6	7	8	9
10	11	12	13	14	15	16
17	18	19	20	21	22	23
24	25	26	27	28	29	30

Do

Weekly Affirmation: _____

Monday	Tuesday	Wednesday
Dinner:	Dinner:	Dinner:
Exercise:	Exercise:	Exercise:

Notes

Water

	1	2	3	4	5	6	7	8
M								
T								
W								
T								
F								
S								
S								

It

Thursday	Friday	Saturday
		Sunday
Dinner:	Dinner:	
Exercise:	Exercise:	

Daily Habits	M	T	W	T	F	S	S

Appointments

Monthly Review

Best

Accomplishments	Significant Events	What brought the most joy?

Worst

Biggest Challenges	Personal Struggles	Changes for Next Month

Truth:

How am I different?

Financial Tracker

Income	
Expenses	
Profit	
Tithe	
Savings	

Weight Tracker

	M	T	W	T	F
Week 1					
Week 2					
Week 3					
Week 4					
Week 5					

Books I Read

I am most proud of:

Ideas & inspiration for next month

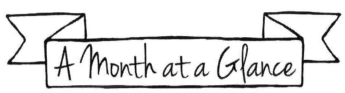

A Month at a Glance

And now let us welcome the new year, full of things that never were.
Lydia Sweatt

Goals: Writing

Week 1: _____
Week 2: _____
Week 3: _____
Week 4: _____
Week 5: _____

Goals: Marketing

Week 1: _____
Week 2: _____
Week 3: _____
Week 4: _____
Week 5: _____

Goals: Craft

Week 1: _____
Week 2: _____
Week 3: _____
Week 4: _____
Week 5: _____

Goals: Other

Week 1: _____
Week 2: _____
Week 3: _____
Week 4: _____
Week 5: _____

Important Dates

_____
_____
_____
_____

Things to Remember:

_____
_____
_____
_____

I AM grateful FOR:

_____
_____
_____
_____

Favorite Writing Quote

July

Sunday	Monday	Tuesday	Wednesday
1	2	3	4
8	9	10	11
15	16	17	18
22	23	24	25
29	30	31	

2018 ◇ ◆ ◇

Thursday	Friday	Saturday	Notes
5	6	7	
12	13	14	
19	20	21	
26	27	28	

Daily

Monday

Verse

Reflection

Truth

Prayers

Tuesday

Verse

Reflection

Truth

Prayers

Wednesday

Verse

Reflection

Truth

Prayers

Thursday

Verse

Reflection

Truth

Prayers

Inspiration

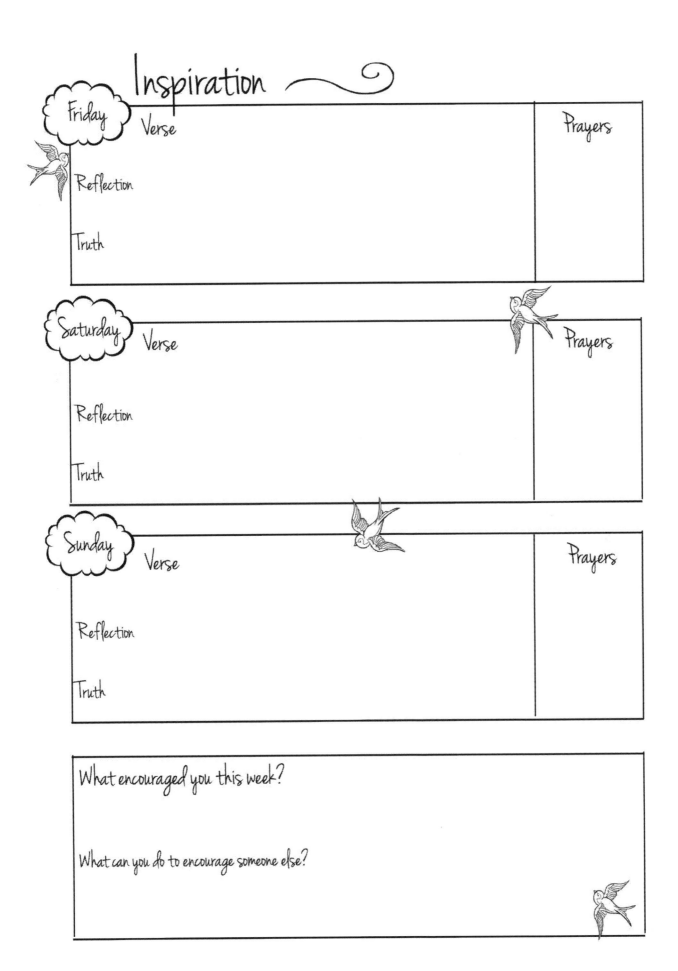

Friday

Verse

Reflection

Truth

Prayers

Saturday

Verse

Reflection

Truth

Prayers

Sunday

Verse

Reflection

Truth

Prayers

What encouraged you this week?

What can you do to encourage someone else?

Make it

Writing

☐
☐
☐
☐
☐
☐
☐

Marketing

☐
☐
☐
☐
☐
☐
☐

Craft

☐
☐
☐
☐
☐
☐
☐

Calls to Make

Errands

Happen

Project

- ☐
- ☐
- ☐
- ☐
- ☐
- ☐
- ☐

Other

- ☐
- ☐
- ☐
- ☐
- ☐
- ☐
- ☐

Menu

Day	
Monday	
Tuesday	
Wednesday	
Thursday	
Friday	
Saturday	
Sunday	

July

S	M	T	W	T	F	S
1	2	3	4	5	6	7
8	9	10	11	12	13	14
15	16	17	18	19	20	21
22	23	24	25	26	27	28
29	30	31				

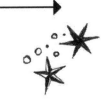

Do

Weekly Affirmation: _____

Monday	Tuesday	Wednesday
Dinner:	Dinner:	Dinner:
Exercise:	Exercise:	Exercise:

Notes

Water

	1	2	3	4	5	6	7	8
M								
T								
W								
T								
F								
S								
S								

It

Thursday	Friday	Saturday

		Sunday

Dinner:

Dinner:

Exercise:

Exercise:

Daily Habits

	M	T	W	T	F	S	S

Appointments

Daily

Monday

Verse

Reflection

Truth

Prayers

Tuesday

Verse

Reflection

Truth

Prayers

Wednesday

Verse

Reflection

Truth

Prayers

Thursday

Verse

Reflection

Truth

Prayers

Inspiration

Friday

Verse

Reflection

Truth

Prayers

Saturday

Verse

Reflection

Truth

Prayers

Sunday

Verse

Reflection

Truth

Prayers

What encouraged you this week?

What can you do to encourage someone else?

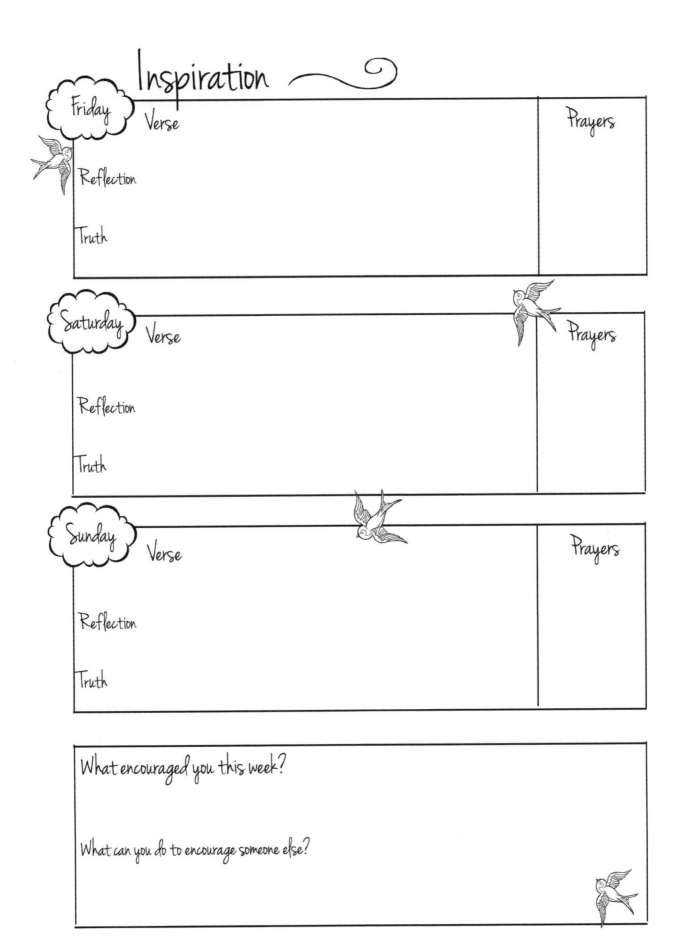

Make it

Writing

- ☐
- ☐
- ☐
- ☐
- ☐
- ☐
- ☐

Marketing

- ☐
- ☐
- ☐
- ☐
- ☐
- ☐
- ☐

Craft

- ☐
- ☐
- ☐
- ☐
- ☐
- ☐
- ☐

Calls to Make

Errands

Happen

Project

- ☐
- ☐
- ☐
- ☐
- ☐
- ☐
- ☐

Other

- ☐
- ☐
- ☐
- ☐
- ☐
- ☐

Menu

Monday	
Tuesday	
Wednesday	
Thursday	
Friday	
Saturday	
Sunday	

July

S	M	T	W	T	F	S
1	2	3	4	5	6	7
8	9	10	11	12	13	14
15	16	17	18	19	20	21
22	23	24	25	26	27	28
29	30	31				

Do

Weekly Affirmation: _____

Monday	Tuesday	Wednesday
Dinner:	Dinner:	Dinner:
Exercise:	Exercise:	Exercise:

Notes

Water

	1	2	3	4	5	6	7	8
M								
T								
W								
T								
F								
S								
S								

It - - - - - - - - - - - ▶

Thursday	Friday	Saturday
		Sunday
Dinner:	Dinner:	
Exercise:	Exercise:	

Daily Habits

	M	T	W	T	F	S	S

Appointments

Daily

Monday

Verse

Reflection

Truth

Prayers

Tuesday

Verse

Reflection

Truth

Prayers

Wednesday

Verse

Reflection

Truth

Prayers

Thursday

Verse

Reflection

Truth

Prayers

Inspiration

Friday

Verse

Reflection

Truth

Prayers

Saturday

Verse

Reflection

Truth

Prayers

Sunday

Verse

Reflection

Truth

Prayers

What encouraged you this week?

What can you do to encourage someone else?

Make it

Writing

- ☐
- ☐
- ☐
- ☐
- ☐
- ☐
- ☐

Marketing

- ☐
- ☐
- ☐
- ☐
- ☐
- ☐
- ☐

Craft

- ☐
- ☐
- ☐
- ☐
- ☐
- ☐
- ☐

Calls to Make

Errands

Happen

Project

- ☐
- ☐
- ☐
- ☐
- ☐
- ☐
- ☐

Other

- ☐
- ☐
- ☐
- ☐
- ☐
- ☐
- ☐

Menu

Monday	
Tuesday	
Wednesday	
Thursday	
Friday	
Saturday	
Sunday	

July

S	M	T	W	T	F	S
1	2	3	4	5	6	7
8	9	10	11	12	13	14
15	16	17	18	19	20	21
22	23	24	25	26	27	28
29	30	31				

Do

Weekly Affirmation: _____

Monday	Tuesday	Wednesday
Dinner:	Dinner:	Dinner:
Exercise:	Exercise:	Exercise:

Notes

Water

	1	2	3	4	5	6	7	8
M								
T								
W								
T								
F								
S								
S								

It ------->

Thursday	Friday	Saturday
		Sunday
Dinner:	Dinner:	
Exercise:	Exercise:	

Daily Habits	M	T	W	T	F	S	S

Appointments

Daily

Monday

Verse

Reflection

Truth

Prayers

Tuesday

Verse

Reflection

Truth

Prayers

Wednesday

Verse

Reflection

Truth

Prayers

Thursday

Verse

Reflection

Truth

Prayers

Inspiration

Friday

Verse

Reflection

Truth

Prayers

Saturday

Verse

Reflection

Truth

Prayers

Sunday

Verse

Reflection

Truth

Prayers

What encouraged you this week?

What can you do to encourage someone else?

Make it

Writing
- ☐
- ☐
- ☐
- ☐
- ☐
- ☐
- ☐

Marketing
- ☐
- ☐
- ☐
- ☐
- ☐
- ☐
- ☐

Craft
- ☐
- ☐
- ☐
- ☐
- ☐
- ☐
- ☐

Calls to Make

Errands

Happen

Project

- ☐
- ☐
- ☐
- ☐
- ☐
- ☐
- ☐

Other

- ☐
- ☐
- ☐
- ☐
- ☐
- ☐
- ☐

Menu

Monday
Tuesday
Wednesday
Thursday
Friday
Saturday
Sunday

July

S	M	T	W	T	F	S
1	2	3	4	5	6	7
8	9	10	11	12	13	14
15	16	17	18	19	20	21
22	23	24	25	26	27	28
29	30	31				

Do

Weekly Affirmation: _____

Monday	Tuesday	Wednesday
Dinner:	Dinner:	Dinner:
Exercise:	Exercise:	Exercise:

Notes

Water

	1	2	3	4	5	6	7	8
M								
T								
W								
T								
F								
S								
S								

It

Thursday	Friday	Saturday

Sunday

Dinner:

Exercise:

Dinner:

Exercise:

Daily Habits

	M	T	W	T	F	S	S

Appointments

Daily

Monday

Verse

Reflection

Truth

Prayers

Tuesday

Verse

Reflection

Truth

Prayers

Wednesday

Verse

Reflection

Truth

Prayers

Thursday

Verse

Reflection

Truth

Prayers

Inspiration

Friday

Verse

Reflection

Truth

Prayers

Saturday

Verse

Reflection

Truth

Prayers

Sunday

Verse

Reflection

Truth

Prayers

What encouraged you this week?

What can you do to encourage someone else?

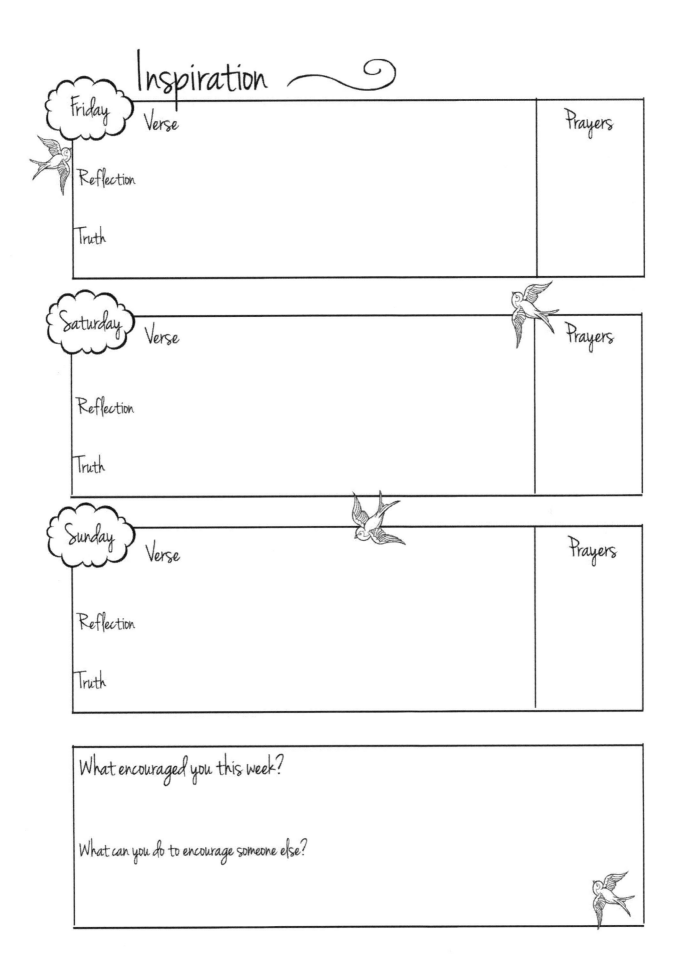

Make it

Writing

- ☐
- ☐
- ☐
- ☐
- ☐
- ☐
- ☐

Marketing

- ☐
- ☐
- ☐
- ☐
- ☐
- ☐
- ☐

Craft

- ☐
- ☐
- ☐
- ☐
- ☐
- ☐
- ☐

Calls to Make

Errands

Happen →

Project

- ☐
- ☐
- ☐
- ☐
- ☐
- ☐
- ☐

Other

- ☐
- ☐
- ☐
- ☐
- ☐
- ☐
- ☐

Menu

Monday

Tuesday

Wednesday

Thursday

Friday

Saturday

Sunday

July

S	M	T	W	T	F	S
1	2	3	4	5	6	7
8	9	10	11	12	13	14
15	16	17	18	19	20	21
22	23	24	25	26	27	28
29	30	31				

Do

Weekly Affirmation: _____

Monday	Tuesday	Wednesday
Dinner:	Dinner:	Dinner:
Exercise:	Exercise:	Exercise:

Notes

Water

	1	2	3	4	5	6	7	8
M								
T								
W								
T								
F								
S								
S								

It - - - - - - - - - - - ▶

Thursday	Friday	Saturday
		Sunday
Dinner:	Dinner:	
Exercise:	Exercise:	

Daily Habits

	M	T	W	T	F	S	S

Appointments

Monthly Review

Best

Accomplishments	Significant Events	What brought the most joy?

Worst

Biggest Challenges	Personal Struggles	Changes for Next Month

Truth:

How am I different?

Financial Tracker

Income	
Expenses	
Profit	
Tithe	
Savings	

Weight Tracker

	M	T	W	T	F
Week 1					
Week 2					
Week 3					
Week 4					
Week 5					

Books I Read

I am most proud of:

Ideas & inspiration for next month

A Month at a Glance

And now let us welcome the new year, full of things that never were.
Lydia Sweatt

Goals: Writing

Week 1: _____

Week 2: _____

Week 3: _____

Week 4: _____

Week 5: _____

Goals: Marketing

Week 1: _____

Week 2: _____

Week 3: _____

Week 4: _____

Week 5: _____

Goals: Craft

Week 1: _____

Week 2: _____

Week 3: _____

Week 4: _____

Week 5: _____

Goals: Other

Week 1: _____

Week 2: _____

Week 3: _____

Week 4: _____

Week 5: _____

Important Dates

_____

_____

_____

_____

Things to Remember:

_____

_____

_____

_____

_____

I AM grateful FOR:

_____

_____

_____

Favorite Writing Quote

August

Sunday	Monday	Tuesday	Wednesday
			1
5	6	7	8
12	13	14	15
19	20	21	22
26	27	28	29

2018 ◇◆◇

Thursday	Friday	Saturday	Notes
2	3	4	
9	10	11	
16	17	18	
23	24	25	
30	31		

Daily

Monday

Verse

Reflection

Truth

Prayers

Tuesday

Verse

Reflection

Truth

Prayers

Wednesday

Verse

Reflection

Truth

Prayers

Thursday

Verse

Reflection

Truth

Prayers

Inspiration

Friday

Verse

Reflection

Truth

Prayers

Saturday

Verse

Reflection

Truth

Prayers

Sunday

Verse

Reflection

Truth

Prayers

What encouraged you this week?

What can you do to encourage someone else?

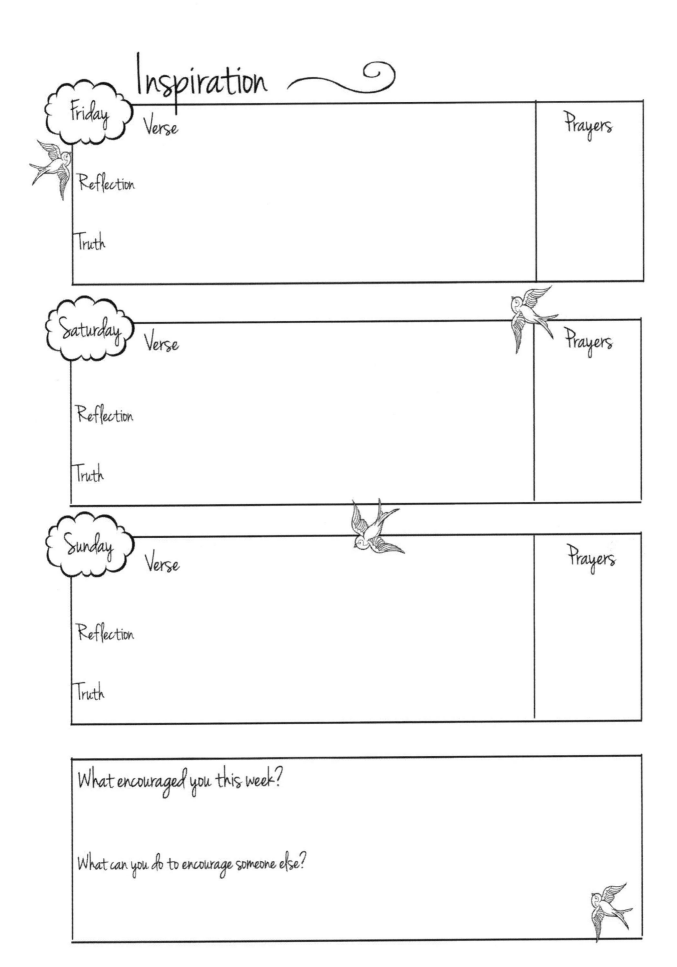

Make it

Writing

- ☐
- ☐
- ☐
- ☐
- ☐
- ☐
- ☐

Marketing

- ☐
- ☐
- ☐
- ☐
- ☐
- ☐
- ☐

Craft

- ☐
- ☐
- ☐
- ☐
- ☐
- ☐
- ☐

Calls to Make

Errands

Happen

Project

- ☐
- ☐
- ☐
- ☐
- ☐
- ☐
- ☐

Other

- ☐
- ☐
- ☐
- ☐
- ☐
- ☐
- ☐

Menu

Monday
Tuesday
Wednesday
Thursday
Friday
Saturday
Sunday

August

S	M	T	W	T	F	S
			1	2	3	4
5	6	7	8	9	10	11
12	13	14	15	16	17	18
19	20	21	22	23	24	25
26	27	28	29	30	31	

Do

Weekly Affirmation: _____

Monday	Tuesday	Wednesday
Dinner:	Dinner:	Dinner:
Exercise:	Exercise:	Exercise:

Notes

Water

	1	2	3	4	5	6	7	8
M								
T								
W								
T								
F								
S								
S								

It

Thursday	Friday	Saturday
Dinner:	Dinner:	**Sunday**
Exercise:	Exercise:	

Daily Habits

	M	T	W	T	F	S	S

Appointments

Daily

Monday

Verse

Reflection

Truth

Prayers

Tuesday

Verse

Reflection

Truth

Prayers

Wednesday

Verse

Reflection

Truth

Prayers

Thursday

Verse

Reflection

Truth

Prayers

Inspiration

Friday

Verse

Reflection

Truth

Prayers

Saturday

Verse

Reflection

Truth

Prayers

Sunday

Verse

Reflection

Truth

Prayers

What encouraged you this week?

What can you do to encourage someone else?

Make it

Writing
- ☐
- ☐
- ☐
- ☐
- ☐
- ☐
- ☐

Marketing
- ☐
- ☐
- ☐
- ☐
- ☐
- ☐
- ☐

Craft
- ☐
- ☐
- ☐
- ☐
- ☐
- ☐
- ☐

Calls to Make

Errands

Happen →

Project

- ☐
- ☐
- ☐
- ☐
- ☐
- ☐
- ☐

Other

- ☐
- ☐
- ☐
- ☐
- ☐
- ☐
- ☐

Menu

Monday

Tuesday

Wednesday

Thursday

Friday

Saturday

Sunday

August

S	M	T	W	T	F	S
			1	2	3	4
5	6	7	8	9	10	11
12	13	14	15	16	17	18
19	20	21	22	23	24	25
26	27	28	29	30	31	

Do

Weekly Affirmation: _____

Monday	Tuesday	Wednesday
Dinner:	Dinner:	Dinner:
Exercise:	Exercise:	Exercise:

Notes

Water

	1	2	3	4	5	6	7	8
M								
T								
W								
T								
F								
S								
S								

It

Thursday	Friday	Saturday
Dinner:	Dinner:	

	Sunday

Dinner:

Exercise:

Dinner:

Exercise:

Daily Habits

	M	T	W	T	F	S	S

Appointments

Daily

Monday

Verse

Prayers

Reflection

Truth

Tuesday

Verse

Prayers

Reflection

Truth

Wednesday

Verse

Prayers

Reflection

Truth

Thursday

Verse

Prayers

Reflection

Truth

Inspiration

Friday

Verse

Reflection

Truth

Prayers

Saturday

Verse

Reflection

Truth

Prayers

Sunday

Verse

Reflection

Truth

Prayers

What encouraged you this week?

What can you do to encourage someone else?

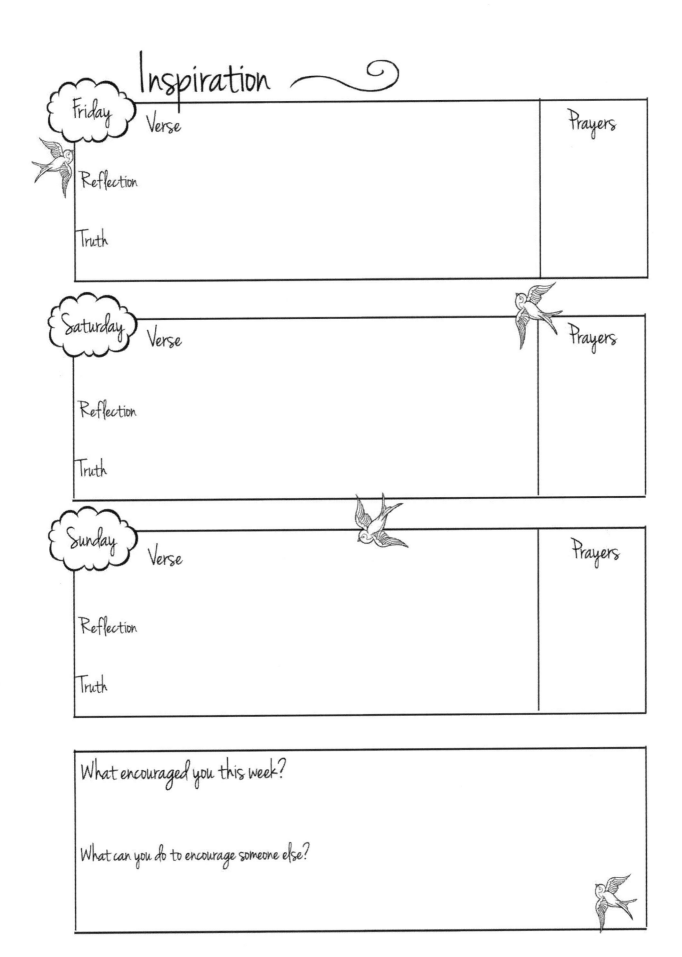

Make it

Writing

☐
☐
☐
☐
☐
☐
☐

Marketing

☐
☐
☐
☐
☐
☐
☐

Craft

☐
☐
☐
☐
☐
☐
☐

Calls to Make

Errands

Happen

Project

- ☐
- ☐
- ☐
- ☐
- ☐
- ☐
- ☐

Other

- ☐
- ☐
- ☐
- ☐
- ☐
- ☐

Menu

Monday
Tuesday
Wednesday
Thursday
Friday
Saturday
Sunday

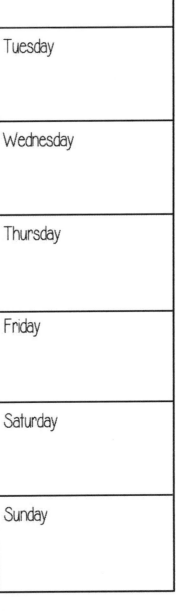

August

S	M	T	W	T	F	S
			1	2	3	4
5	6	7	8	9	10	11
12	13	14	15	16	17	18
19	20	21	22	23	24	25
26	27	28	29	30	31	

Do

Weekly Affirmation: _____

Monday	Tuesday	Wednesday
Dinner:	Dinner:	Dinner:
Exercise:	Exercise:	Exercise:

Notes

Water

	1	2	3	4	5	6	7	8
M								
T								
W								
T								
F								
S								
S								

It

Thursday	Friday	Saturday

Dinner:

Dinner:

| | | Sunday |

Exercise:

Exercise:

Daily Habits	M	T	W	T	F	S	S

Appointments

Daily

Monday

Verse

Reflection

Truth

Prayers

Tuesday

Verse

Reflection

Truth

Prayers

Wednesday

Verse

Reflection

Truth

Prayers

Thursday

Verse

Reflection

Truth

Prayers

Inspiration

Friday

Verse

Prayers

Reflection

Truth

Saturday

Verse

Prayers

Reflection

Truth

Sunday

Verse

Prayers

Reflection

Truth

What encouraged you this week?

What can you do to encourage someone else?

Make it

Writing
☐
☐
☐
☐
☐
☐
☐

Marketing
☐
☐
☐
☐
☐
☐
☐

Craft
☐
☐
☐
☐
☐
☐
☐

Calls to Make

Errands

Happen

Project

- ☐
- ☐
- ☐
- ☐
- ☐
- ☐
- ☐

Other

- ☐
- ☐
- ☐
- ☐
- ☐
- ☐
- ☐

Menu

| Monday |
| Tuesday |
| Wednesday |
| Thursday |
| Friday |
| Saturday |
| Sunday |

August

S	M	T	W	T	F	S
			1	2	3	4
5	6	7	8	9	10	11
12	13	14	15	16	17	18
19	20	21	22	23	24	25
26	27	28	29	30	31	

Do

Weekly Affirmation: _____

Monday	Tuesday	Wednesday
Dinner:	Dinner:	Dinner:
Exercise:	Exercise:	Exercise:

Notes

Water

	1	2	3	4	5	6	7	8
M								
T								
W								
T								
F								
S								
S								

It

Thursday	Friday	Saturday

Dinner: Dinner:

Exercise: Exercise:

Sunday

Daily Habits	M	T	W	T	F	S	S

Appointments

Monday

Verse

Prayers

Reflection

Truth

Tuesday

Verse

Prayers

Reflection

Truth

Wednesday

Verse

Prayers

Reflection

Truth

Thursday

Verse

Prayers

Reflection

Truth

Inspiration

Friday

Verse

Reflection

Truth

Prayers

Saturday

Verse

Reflection

Truth

Prayers

Sunday

Verse

Reflection

Truth

Prayers

What encouraged you this week?

What can you do to encourage someone else?

Make it

Writing
- [ ]
- [ ]
- [ ]
- [ ]
- [ ]
- [ ]
- [ ]

Marketing
- [ ]
- [ ]
- [ ]
- [ ]
- [ ]
- [ ]
- [ ]

Craft
- [ ]
- [ ]
- [ ]
- [ ]
- [ ]
- [ ]
- [ ]

Calls to Make

Errands

Happen

Project

- ☐
- ☐
- ☐
- ☐
- ☐
- ☐
- ☐

Other

- ☐
- ☐
- ☐
- ☐
- ☐
- ☐
- ☐

Menu

Monday
Tuesday
Wednesday
Thursday
Friday
Saturday
Sunday

August

S	M	T	W	T	F	S
			1	2	3	4
5	6	7	8	9	10	11
12	13	14	15	16	17	18
19	20	21	22	23	24	25
26	27	28	29	30	31	

Weekly Affirmation: _____

Monday	Tuesday	Wednesday
Dinner:	Dinner:	Dinner:
Exercise:	Exercise:	Exercise:

Notes

Water

	1	2	3	4	5	6	7	8
M								
T								
W								
T								
F								
S								
S								

It

Thursday	Friday	Saturday

Sunday

Dinner:

Exercise:

Dinner:

Exercise:

Daily Habits	M	T	W	T	F	S	S

Appointments

Monthly Review

Best

Accomplishments	Significant Events	What brought the most joy?

Worst

Biggest Challenges	Personal Struggles	Changes for Next Month

Truth:

How am I different?

Financial Tracker

Income	
Expenses	
Profit	
Tithe	
Savings	

Weight Tracker

	M	T	W	T	F
Week 1					
Week 2					
Week 3					
Week 4					
Week 5					

Books I Read

I am most proud of:

Ideas & inspiration for next month

A Month at a Glance

And now let us welcome the new year, full of things that never were.
Lydia Sweatt

Goals: Writing

Week 1: _____

Week 2: _____

Week 3: _____

Week 4: _____

Week 5: _____

Goals: Marketing

Week 1: _____

Week 2: _____

Week 3: _____

Week 4: _____

Week 5: _____

Goals: Craft

Week 1: _____

Week 2: _____

Week 3: _____

Week 4: _____

Week 5: _____

Goals: Other

Week 1: _____

Week 2: _____

Week 3: _____

Week 4: _____

Week 5: _____

Important Dates

_____

_____

_____

_____

Things to Remember:

_____

_____

_____

_____

I AM grateful FOR:

_____

_____

_____

Favorite Writing Quote

September

Sunday	Monday	Tuesday	Wednesday
2	3	4	5
9	10	11	12
16	17	18	19
23	24	25	26
30			

2018 ◇◆◇

Thursday	Friday	Saturday	Notes
		1	
6	7	8	
13	14	15	
20	21	22	
27	28	29	

Daily

Monday

Verse

Reflection

Truth

Prayers

Tuesday

Verse

Reflection

Truth

Prayers

Wednesday

Verse

Reflection

Truth

Prayers

Thursday

Verse

Reflection

Truth

Prayers

Inspiration

Friday

Verse

Reflection

Truth

Prayers

Saturday

Verse

Reflection

Truth

Prayers

Sunday

Verse

Reflection

Truth

Prayers

What encouraged you this week?

What can you do to encourage someone else?

Make it

Writing
- ☐
- ☐
- ☐
- ☐
- ☐
- ☐
- ☐

Marketing
- ☐
- ☐
- ☐
- ☐
- ☐
- ☐
- ☐

Craft
- ☐
- ☐
- ☐
- ☐
- ☐
- ☐
- ☐

Calls to Make

Errands

Happen

Project

- ☐
- ☐
- ☐
- ☐
- ☐
- ☐
- ☐

Other

- ☐
- ☐
- ☐
- ☐
- ☐
- ☐
- ☐

Menu

Monday	
Tuesday	
Wednesday	
Thursday	
Friday	
Saturday	
Sunday	

September

S	M	T	W	T	F	S
						1
2	3	4	5	6	7	8
9	10	11	12	13	14	15
16	17	18	19	20	21	22
23	24	25	26	27	28	29
30						

Do

Weekly Affirmation: _____

Monday	Tuesday	Wednesday
Dinner:	Dinner:	Dinner:
Exercise:	Exercise:	Exercise:

Notes

Water							
	1	2	3	4	5	6	7	8
M								
T								
W								
T								
F								
S								
S								

It

Thursday	Friday	Saturday
Dinner:	Dinner:	Sunday
Exercise:	Exercise:	

Daily Habits

	M	T	W	T	F	S	S

Appointments

Daily

Monday

Verse

Reflection

Truth

Prayers

Tuesday

Verse

Reflection

Truth

Prayers

Wednesday

Verse

Reflection

Truth

Prayers

Thursday

Verse

Reflection

Truth

Prayers

Inspiration

Friday

Verse

Reflection

Truth

Prayers

Saturday

Verse

Reflection

Truth

Prayers

Sunday

Verse

Reflection

Truth

Prayers

What encouraged you this week?

What can you do to encourage someone else?

Make it

Writing
- ☐
- ☐
- ☐
- ☐
- ☐
- ☐
- ☐

Marketing
- ☐
- ☐
- ☐
- ☐
- ☐
- ☐
- ☐

Craft
- ☐
- ☐
- ☐
- ☐
- ☐
- ☐
- ☐

Calls to Make

Errands

Happen

Project

- ☐
- ☐
- ☐
- ☐
- ☐
- ☐
- ☐

Other

- ☐
- ☐
- ☐
- ☐
- ☐
- ☐
- ☐

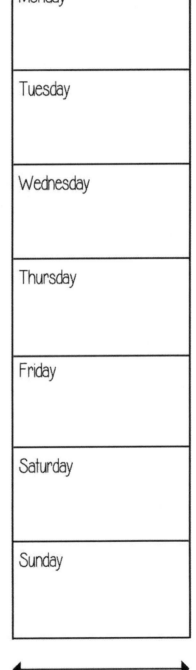

Menu

Monday
Tuesday
Wednesday
Thursday
Friday
Saturday
Sunday

September

S	M	T	W	T	F	S
						1
2	3	4	5	6	7	8
9	10	11	12	13	14	15
16	17	18	19	20	21	22
23	24	25	26	27	28	29
30						

Do

Weekly Affirmation: _____

Monday	Tuesday	Wednesday
Dinner:	Dinner:	Dinner:
Exercise:	Exercise:	Exercise:

Notes

Water

	1	2	3	4	5	6	7	8
M								
T								
W								
T								
F								
S								
S								

It

Thursday	Friday	Saturday
Dinner:	Dinner:	**Sunday**
Exercise:	Exercise:	

Daily Habits	M	T	W	T	F	S	S

Appointments

Daily

Monday

Verse

Reflection

Truth

Prayers

Tuesday

Verse

Reflection

Truth

Prayers

Wednesday

Verse

Reflection

Truth

Prayers

Thursday

Verse

Reflection

Truth

Prayers

Inspiration

Friday

Verse

Reflection

Truth

Prayers

Saturday

Verse

Reflection

Truth

Prayers

Sunday

Verse

Reflection

Truth

Prayers

What encouraged you this week?

What can you do to encourage someone else?

Make it

Writing

☐

☐

☐

☐

☐

☐

☐

Marketing

☐

☐

☐

☐

☐

☐

☐

Craft

☐

☐

☐

☐

☐

☐

☐

Calls to Make

Errands

Happen

Project

- ☐
- ☐
- ☐
- ☐
- ☐
- ☐
- ☐

Other

- ☐
- ☐
- ☐
- ☐
- ☐
- ☐

Menu

Monday
Tuesday
Wednesday
Thursday
Friday
Saturday
Sunday

September

S	M	T	W	T	F	S
						1
2	3	4	5	6	7	8
9	10	11	12	13	14	15
16	17	18	19	20	21	22
23	24	25	26	27	28	29
30						

Do

Weekly Affirmation: _____

Monday	Tuesday	Wednesday
Dinner:	Dinner:	Dinner:
Exercise:	Exercise:	Exercise:

Notes

Water

	1	2	3	4	5	6	7	8
M								
T								
W								
T								
F								
S								
S								

It

Thursday	Friday	Saturday

Sunday

Dinner:

Dinner:

Exercise:

Exercise:

Daily Habits

	M	T	W	T	F	S	S

Appointments

Daily

Monday

Verse

Reflection

Truth

Prayers

Tuesday

Verse

Reflection

Truth

Prayers

Wednesday

Verse

Reflection

Truth

Prayers

Thursday

Verse

Reflection

Truth

Prayers

Inspiration

Friday

Verse

Reflection

Truth

Prayers

Saturday

Verse

Reflection

Truth

Prayers

Sunday

Verse

Reflection

Truth

Prayers

What encouraged you this week?

What can you do to encourage someone else?

Make it

Writing

- ☐
- ☐
- ☐
- ☐
- ☐
- ☐
- ☐

Marketing

- ☐
- ☐
- ☐
- ☐
- ☐
- ☐
- ☐

Craft

- ☐
- ☐
- ☐
- ☐
- ☐
- ☐
- ☐

Calls to Make

Errands

Happen

Project

- ☐
- ☐
- ☐
- ☐
- ☐
- ☐
- ☐

Other

- ☐
- ☐
- ☐
- ☐
- ☐
- ☐

Menu

Monday

Tuesday

Wednesday

Thursday

Friday

Saturday

Sunday

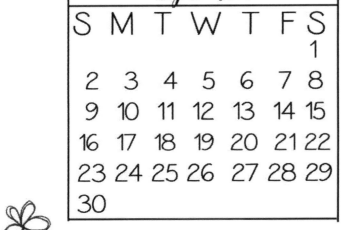

September

S	M	T	W	T	F	S
						1
2	3	4	5	6	7	8
9	10	11	12	13	14	15
16	17	18	19	20	21	22
23	24	25	26	27	28	29
30						

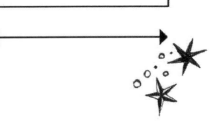

Weekly Affirmation: _____

Monday	Tuesday	Wednesday
Dinner:	Dinner:	Dinner:
Exercise:	Exercise:	Exercise:

Notes

Water

	1	2	3	4	5	6	7	8
M								
T								
W								
T								
F								
S								
S								

It ------►

Thursday	Friday	Saturday
Dinner:	Dinner:	

Sunday

Daily Habits

	M	T	W	T	F	S	S

Appointments

Daily

Monday

Verse

Reflection

Truth

Prayers

Tuesday

Verse

Reflection

Truth

Prayers

Wednesday

Verse

Reflection

Truth

Prayers

Thursday

Verse

Reflection

Truth

Prayers

Inspiration

Friday

Verse

Prayers

Reflection

Truth

Saturday

Verse

Prayers

Reflection

Truth

Sunday

Verse

Prayers

Reflection

Truth

What encouraged you this week?

What can you do to encourage someone else?

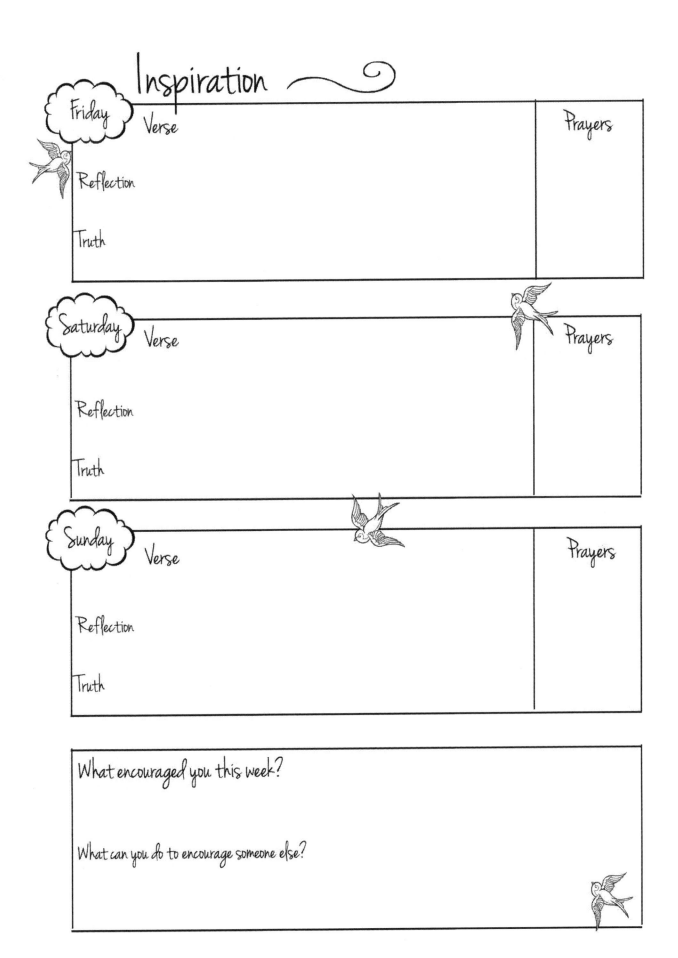

Make it

Writing

- ☐
- ☐
- ☐
- ☐
- ☐
- ☐
- ☐

Marketing

- ☐
- ☐
- ☐
- ☐
- ☐
- ☐
- ☐

Craft

- ☐
- ☐
- ☐
- ☐
- ☐
- ☐
- ☐

Calls to Make

Errands

Happen

Project

- [ ]
- [ ]
- [ ]
- [ ]
- [ ]
- [ ]
- [ ]

Other

- [ ]
- [ ]
- [ ]
- [ ]
- [ ]
- [ ]
- [ ]

Menu

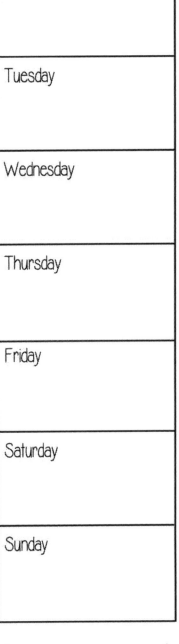

Monday

Tuesday

Wednesday

Thursday

Friday

Saturday

Sunday

September

S	M	T	W	T	F	S
						1
2	3	4	5	6	7	8
9	10	11	12	13	14	15
16	17	18	19	20	21	22
23	24	25	26	27	28	29
30						

Do

Weekly Affirmation: _____

Monday	Tuesday	Wednesday
Dinner:	Dinner:	Dinner:
Exercise:	Exercise:	Exercise:

Notes

Water

	1	2	3	4	5	6	7	8
M								
T								
W								
T								
F								
S								
S								

It

Thursday	Friday	Saturday

		Sunday
Dinner:	Dinner:	
Exercise:	Exercise:	

Daily Habits	M	T	W	T	F	S	S

Appointments

Monthly Review

Best

Accomplishments	Significant Events	What brought the most joy?

Worst

Biggest Challenges	Personal Struggles	Changes for Next Month

Truth:

How am I different?

Financial Tracker

Income	
Expenses	
Profit	
Tithe	
Savings	

Weight Tracker

	M	T	W	T	F
Week 1					
Week 2					
Week 3					
Week 4					
Week 5					

Books I Read

I am most proud of:

Ideas & inspiration for next month

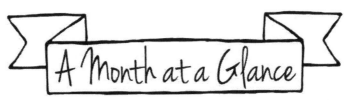

A Month at a Glance

And now let us welcome the new year, full of things that never were.
Lydia Sweatt

Goals: Writing

Week 1: _____
Week 2: _____
Week 3: _____
Week 4: _____
Week 5: _____

Goals: Marketing

Week 1: _____
Week 2: _____
Week 3: _____
Week 4: _____
Week 5: _____

Goals: Craft

Week 1: _____
Week 2: _____
Week 3: _____
Week 4: _____
Week 5: _____

Goals: Other

Week 1: _____
Week 2: _____
Week 3: _____
Week 4: _____
Week 5: _____

Important Dates

_____
_____
_____
_____

Things to Remember:

_____
_____
_____
_____

I AM grateful FOR:

_____
_____
_____

Favorite Writing Quote

October

Sunday	Monday	Tuesday	Wednesday
	1	2	3
7	8	9	10
14	15	16	17
21	22	23	24
28	29	30	31

2018 ◇◆◇

Thursday	Friday	Saturday	Notes
4	5	6	
11	12	13	
18	19	20	
25	26	27	

Daily

Monday

Verse

Reflection

Truth

Prayers

Tuesday

Verse

Reflection

Truth

Prayers

Wednesday

Verse

Reflection

Truth

Prayers

Thursday

Verse

Reflection

Truth

Prayers

Inspiration

Friday

Verse

Reflection

Truth

Prayers

Saturday

Verse

Reflection

Truth

Prayers

Sunday

Verse

Reflection

Truth

Prayers

What encouraged you this week?

What can you do to encourage someone else?

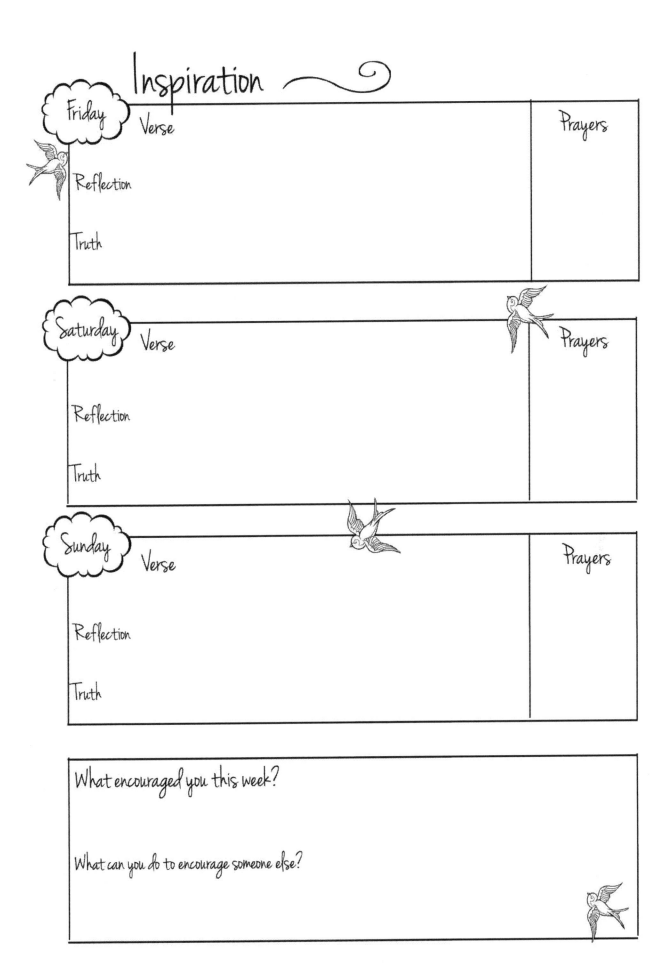

Make it

Writing
☐
☐
☐
☐
☐
☐
☐

Marketing
☐
☐
☐
☐
☐
☐
☐

Craft
☐
☐
☐
☐
☐
☐
☐

Calls to Make

Errands

Happen

Project

- ☐
- ☐
- ☐
- ☐
- ☐
- ☐
- ☐

Other

- ☐
- ☐
- ☐
- ☐
- ☐
- ☐
- ☐

Menu

Monday	
Tuesday	
Wednesday	
Thursday	
Friday	
Saturday	
Sunday	

October

S	M	T	W	T	F	S
	1	2	3	4	5	6
7	8	9	10	11	12	13
14	15	16	17	18	19	20
21	22	23	24	25	26	27
28	29	30	31			

Do

Weekly Affirmation: _____

Monday	Tuesday	Wednesday
Dinner:	Dinner:	Dinner:
Exercise:	Exercise:	Exercise:

Notes

Water

	1	2	3	4	5	6	7	8
M								
T								
W								
T								
F								
S								
S								

It

Thursday	Friday	Saturday

Dinner:

Dinner:

Exercise:

Exercise:

Sunday

Daily Habits

	M	T	W	T	F	S	S

Appointments

Daily

Monday

Verse

Reflection

Truth

Prayers

Tuesday

Verse

Reflection

Truth

Prayers

Wednesday

Verse

Reflection

Truth

Prayers

Thursday

Verse

Reflection

Truth

Prayers

Inspiration

Friday

Verse

Reflection

Truth

Prayers

Saturday

Verse

Reflection

Truth

Prayers

Sunday

Verse

Reflection

Truth

Prayers

What encouraged you this week?

What can you do to encourage someone else?

Make it

Writing	Marketing	Craft
☐	☐	☐
☐	☐	☐
☐	☐	☐
☐	☐	☐
☐	☐	☐
☐	☐	☐
☐	☐	☐

Calls to Make

Errands

Happen

Project

- [ ]
- [ ]
- [ ]
- [ ]
- [ ]
- [ ]
- [ ]

Other

- [ ]
- [ ]
- [ ]
- [ ]
- [ ]
- [ ]

Menu

Monday
Tuesday
Wednesday
Thursday
Friday
Saturday
Sunday

October

S	M	T	W	T	F	S
	1	2	3	4	5	6
7	8	9	10	11	12	13
14	15	16	17	18	19	20
21	22	23	24	25	26	27
28	29	30	31			

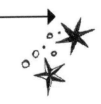

Do

Weekly Affirmation: _____

Monday	Tuesday	Wednesday
Dinner:	Dinner:	Dinner:
Exercise:	Exercise:	Exercise:

Notes

Water

	1	2	3	4	5	6	7	8
M								
T								
W								
T								
F								
S								
S								

It

Thursday	Friday	Saturday

Dinner:

Dinner:

	Sunday

Exercise:

Exercise:

Daily Habits

	M	T	W	T	F	S	S

Appointments

Daily

Monday

Verse

Reflection

Truth

Prayers

Tuesday

Verse

Reflection

Truth

Prayers

Wednesday

Verse

Reflection

Truth

Prayers

Thursday

Verse

Reflection

Truth

Prayers

Inspiration

Friday

Verse

Reflection

Truth

Prayers

Saturday

Verse

Reflection

Truth

Prayers

Sunday

Verse

Reflection

Truth

Prayers

What encouraged you this week?

What can you do to encourage someone else?

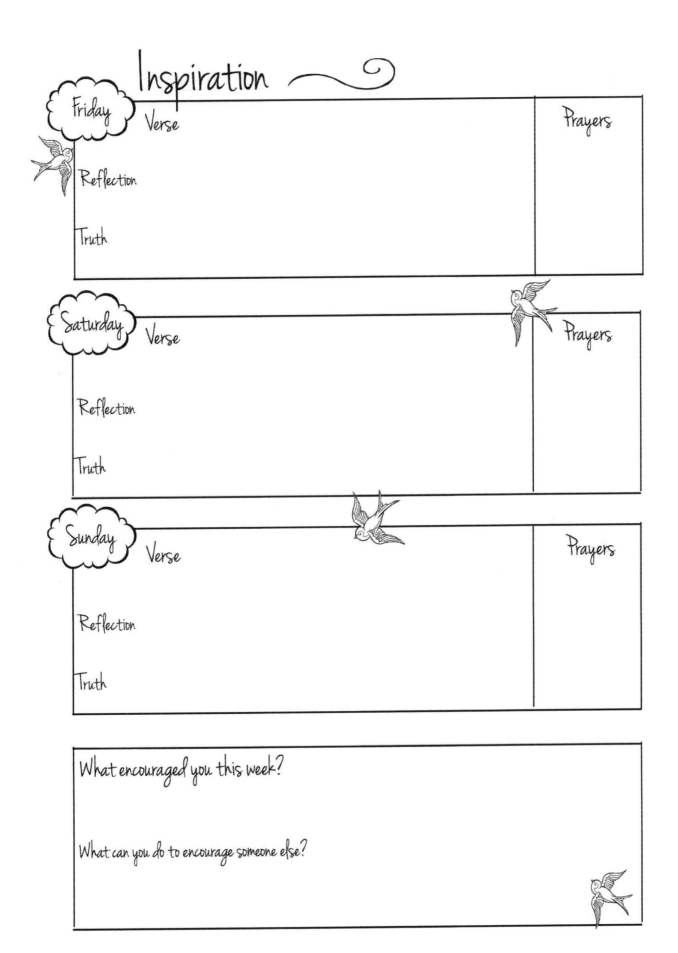

Make it

Writing

☐
☐
☐
☐
☐
☐
☐

Marketing

☐
☐
☐
☐
☐
☐
☐

Craft

☐
☐
☐
☐
☐
☐
☐

Calls to Make

Errands

Happen

Project

- [ ]
- [ ]
- [ ]
- [ ]
- [ ]
- [ ]
- [ ]

Other

- [ ]
- [ ]
- [ ]
- [ ]
- [ ]
- [ ]

Menu

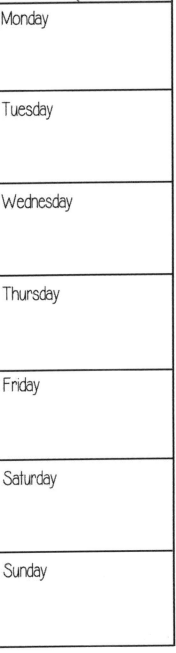

Monday

Tuesday

Wednesday

Thursday

Friday

Saturday

Sunday

October

S	M	T	W	T	F	S
	1	2	3	4	5	6
7	8	9	10	11	12	13
14	15	16	17	18	19	20
21	22	23	24	25	26	27
28	29	30	31			

Do

Weekly Affirmation: _____

Monday	Tuesday	Wednesday
Dinner:	Dinner:	Dinner:
Exercise:	Exercise:	Exercise:

Notes

Water

	1	2	3	4	5	6	7	8
M								
T								
W								
T								
F								
S								
S								

It

Thursday	Friday	Saturday

		Sunday

Dinner:

Dinner:

Exercise:

Exercise:

Daily Habits

	M	T	W	T	F	S	S

Appointments

Daily

Monday

Verse

Reflection

Truth

Prayers

Tuesday

Verse

Reflection

Truth

Prayers

Wednesday

Verse

Reflection

Truth

Prayers

Thursday

Verse

Reflection

Truth

Prayers

Inspiration

Friday

Verse

Reflection

Truth

Prayers

Saturday

Verse

Reflection

Truth

Prayers

Sunday

Verse

Reflection

Truth

Prayers

What encouraged you this week?

What can you do to encourage someone else?

Make it

Writing	Marketing	Craft
☐	☐	☐
☐	☐	☐
☐	☐	☐
☐	☐	☐
☐	☐	☐
☐	☐	☐
☐	☐	☐

Calls to Make

Errands

Happen

Project

- ☐
- ☐
- ☐
- ☐
- ☐
- ☐
- ☐

Other

- ☐
- ☐
- ☐
- ☐
- ☐
- ☐
- ☐

Menu

Monday

Tuesday

Wednesday

Thursday

Friday

Saturday

Sunday

October

S	M	T	W	T	F	S
	1	2	3	4	5	6
7	8	9	10	11	12	13
14	15	16	17	18	19	20
21	22	23	24	25	26	27
28	29	30	31			

Do

Weekly Affirmation: _____

Monday	Tuesday	Wednesday
Dinner:	Dinner:	Dinner:
Exercise:	Exercise:	Exercise:

Notes

Water

	1	2	3	4	5	6	7	8
M								
T								
W								
T								
F								
S								
S								

It - - - - - - - - ➤

Thursday	Friday	Saturday

Dinner:

Dinner:

Sunday

Exercise:

Exercise:

Daily Habits

	M	T	W	T	F	S	S

Appointments

Daily

Monday

Verse

Reflection

Truth

Prayers

Tuesday

Verse

Reflection

Truth

Prayers

Wednesday

Verse

Reflection

Truth

Prayers

Thursday

Verse

Reflection

Truth

Prayers

Inspiration

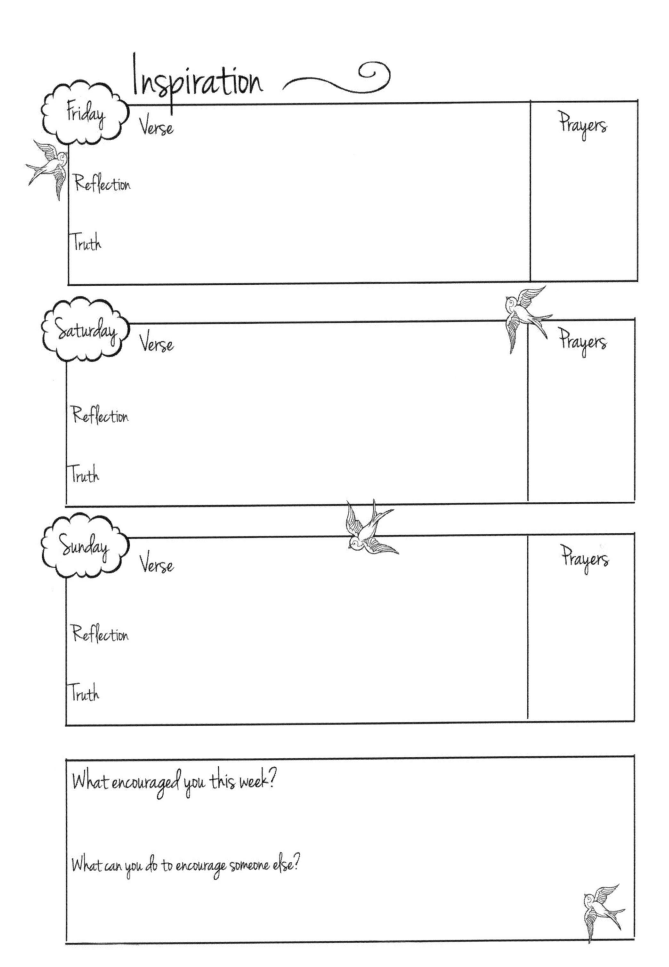

Friday

Verse

Reflection

Truth

Prayers

Saturday

Verse

Reflection

Truth

Prayers

Sunday

Verse

Reflection

Truth

Prayers

What encouraged you this week?

What can you do to encourage someone else?

Make it

Writing

- ☐
- ☐
- ☐
- ☐
- ☐
- ☐
- ☐

Marketing

- ☐
- ☐
- ☐
- ☐
- ☐
- ☐
- ☐

Craft

- ☐
- ☐
- ☐
- ☐
- ☐
- ☐
- ☐

Calls to Make

Errands

Happen

Project

- ☐
- ☐
- ☐
- ☐
- ☐
- ☐
- ☐

Other

- ☐
- ☐
- ☐
- ☐
- ☐
- ☐
- ☐

Menu

Monday

Tuesday

Wednesday

Thursday

Friday

Saturday

Sunday

October

S	M	T	W	T	F	S
	1	2	3	4	5	6
7	8	9	10	11	12	13
14	15	16	17	18	19	20
21	22	23	24	25	26	27
28	29	30	31			

Weekly Affirmation: _____

Monday	Tuesday	Wednesday
Dinner:	Dinner:	Dinner:
Exercise:	Exercise:	Exercise:

Notes

Water

	1	2	3	4	5	6	7	8
M								
T								
W								
T								
F								
S								
S								

It

Thursday	Friday	Saturday
		Sunday
Dinner:	Dinner:	
Exercise:	Exercise:	

Daily Habits	M	T	W	T	F	S	S

Appointments

Monthly Review

Best

Accomplishments	Significant Events	What brought the most joy?

Worst

Biggest Challenges	Personal Struggles	Changes for Next Month

Truth:

How am I different?

Financial Tracker

Income	
Expenses	
Profit	
Tithe	
Savings	

Weight Tracker

	M	T	W	T	F
Week 1					
Week 2					
Week 3					
Week 4					
Week 5					

Books I Read

I am most proud of:

Ideas & inspiration for next month

A Month at a Glance

And now let us welcome the new year, full of things that never were.
Lydia Sweatt

Goals: Writing

Week 1: _____
Week 2: _____
Week 3: _____
Week 4: _____
Week 5: _____

Goals: Marketing

Week 1: _____
Week 2: _____
Week 3: _____
Week 4: _____
Week 5: _____

Goals: Craft

Week 1: _____
Week 2: _____
Week 3: _____
Week 4: _____
Week 5: _____

Goals: Other

Week 1: _____
Week 2: _____
Week 3: _____
Week 4: _____
Week 5: _____

Important Dates

_____
_____
_____
_____
_____

Things to Remember:

_____
_____
_____
_____
_____

I AM grateful FOR:

_____
_____
_____

Favorite Writing Quote

[ ]

November

Sunday	Monday	Tuesday	Wednesday
4	5	6	7
11	12	13	14
18	19	20	21
25	26	27	28

2018 ◇◆◇

Thursday	Friday	Saturday	Notes
1	2	3	
8	9	10	
15	16	17	
22	23	24	
29	30		

Daily

Monday

Verse

Reflection

Truth

Prayers

Tuesday

Verse

Reflection

Truth

Prayers

Wednesday

Verse

Reflection

Truth

Prayers

Thursday

Verse

Reflection

Truth

Prayers

Inspiration

Friday

Verse

Reflection

Truth

Prayers

Saturday

Verse

Reflection

Truth

Prayers

Sunday

Verse

Reflection

Truth

Prayers

What encouraged you this week?

What can you do to encourage someone else?

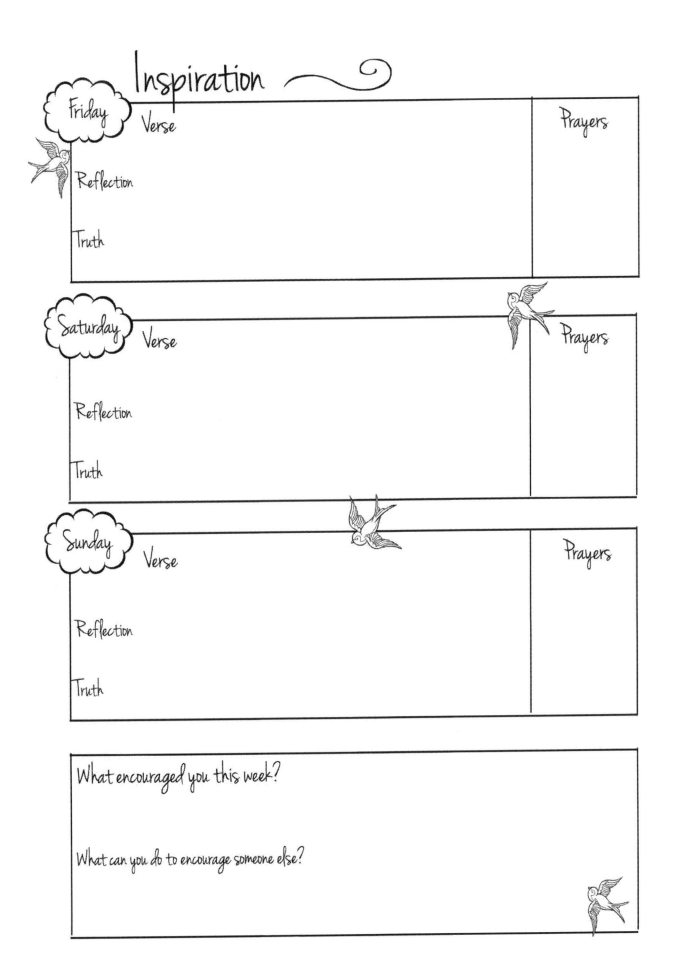

Make it

Writing
- ☐
- ☐
- ☐
- ☐
- ☐
- ☐
- ☐

Marketing
- ☐
- ☐
- ☐
- ☐
- ☐
- ☐
- ☐

Craft
- ☐
- ☐
- ☐
- ☐
- ☐
- ☐
- ☐

Calls to Make

Errands

Happen

Project

- ☐
- ☐
- ☐
- ☐
- ☐
- ☐
- ☐

Other

- ☐
- ☐
- ☐
- ☐
- ☐
- ☐
- ☐

Menu

Monday
Tuesday
Wednesday
Thursday
Friday
Saturday
Sunday

November

S	M	T	W	T	F	S
				1	2	3
4	5	6	7	8	9	10
11	12	13	14	15	16	17
18	19	20	21	22	23	24
25	26	27	28	29	30	

Do

Weekly Affirmation: _____

Monday	Tuesday	Wednesday
Dinner:	Dinner:	Dinner:
Exercise:	Exercise:	Exercise:

Notes

Water

	1	2	3	4	5	6	7	8
M								
T								
W								
T								
F								
S								
S								

It

Thursday	Friday	Saturday

Sunday

Dinner:

Dinner:

Exercise:

Exercise:

Daily Habits

	M	T	W	T	F	S	S

Appointments

Daily

Monday

Verse

Reflection

Truth

Prayers

Tuesday

Verse

Reflection

Truth

Prayers

Wednesday

Verse

Reflection

Truth

Prayers

Thursday

Verse

Reflection

Truth

Prayers

Inspiration

Friday

Verse

Reflection

Truth

Prayers

Saturday

Verse

Reflection

Truth

Prayers

Sunday

Verse

Reflection

Truth

Prayers

What encouraged you this week?

What can you do to encourage someone else?

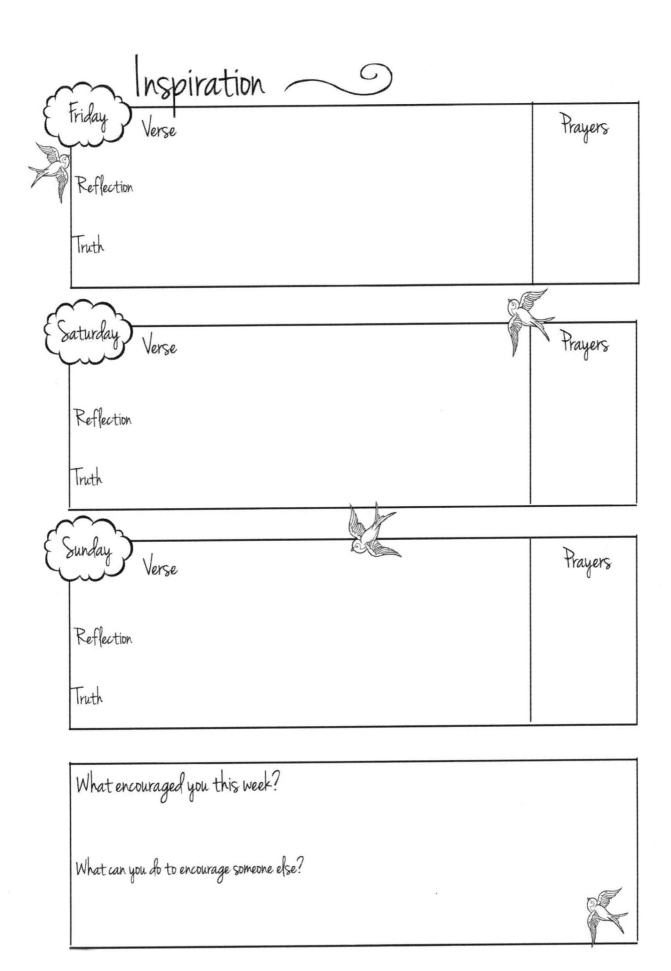

Make it

Writing

☐
☐
☐
☐
☐
☐
☐

Marketing

☐
☐
☐
☐
☐
☐
☐

Craft

☐
☐
☐
☐
☐
☐
☐

Calls to Make

Errands

Happen

Project

- ☐
- ☐
- ☐
- ☐
- ☐
- ☐
- ☐

Other

- ☐
- ☐
- ☐
- ☐
- ☐
- ☐

Menu

Monday	
Tuesday	
Wednesday	
Thursday	
Friday	
Saturday	
Sunday	

November

S	M	T	W	T	F	S
				1	2	3
4	5	6	7	8	9	10
11	12	13	14	15	16	17
18	19	20	21	22	23	24
25	26	27	28	29	30	

Do

Weekly Affirmation: _____

Monday	Tuesday	Wednesday
Dinner:	Dinner:	Dinner:
Exercise:	Exercise:	Exercise:

Notes

Water

	1	2	3	4	5	6	7	8
M								
T								
W								
T								
F								
S								
S								

It

Thursday	Friday	Saturday
		Sunday
Dinner:	Dinner:	
Exercise:	Exercise:	

Daily Habits

	M	T	W	T	F	S	S

Appointments

Daily

Monday
Verse

Reflection

Truth

Prayers

Tuesday
Verse

Reflection

Truth

Prayers

Wednesday
Verse

Reflection

Truth

Prayers

Thursday
Verse

Reflection

Truth

Prayers

Inspiration

Friday

Verse

Reflection

Truth

Prayers

Saturday

Verse

Reflection

Truth

Prayers

Sunday

Verse

Reflection

Truth

Prayers

What encouraged you this week?

What can you do to encourage someone else?

Make it

Writing	Marketing	Craft
☐	☐	☐
☐	☐	☐
☐	☐	☐
☐	☐	☐
☐	☐	☐
☐	☐	☐
☐	☐	☐

Calls to Make

Errands

Happen

Project

- ☐
- ☐
- ☐
- ☐
- ☐
- ☐
- ☐

Other

- ☐
- ☐
- ☐
- ☐
- ☐
- ☐
- ☐

Menu

Monday
Tuesday
Wednesday
Thursday
Friday
Saturday
Sunday

November

S	M	T	W	T	F	S
				1	2	3
4	5	6	7	8	9	10
11	12	13	14	15	16	17
18	19	20	21	22	23	24
25	26	27	28	29	30	

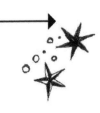

Weekly Affirmation: _____

Monday	Tuesday	Wednesday
Dinner:	Dinner:	Dinner:
Exercise:	Exercise:	Exercise:

Notes

Water

	1	2	3	4	5	6	7	8
M								
T								
W								
T								
F								
S								
S								

It

Thursday	Friday	Saturday

		Sunday

Dinner:

Dinner:

Exercise:

Exercise:

Daily Habits

	M	T	W	T	F	S	S

Appointments

Daily

Monday

Verse

Reflection

Truth

Prayers

Tuesday

Verse

Reflection

Truth

Prayers

Wednesday

Verse

Reflection

Truth

Prayers

Thursday

Verse

Reflection

Truth

Prayers

Inspiration

Friday

Verse

Reflection

Truth

Prayers

Saturday

Verse

Reflection

Truth

Prayers

Sunday

Verse

Reflection

Truth

Prayers

What encouraged you this week?

What can you do to encourage someone else?

Make it

Writing

☐
☐
☐
☐
☐
☐
☐

Marketing

☐
☐
☐
☐
☐
☐
☐

Craft

☐
☐
☐
☐
☐
☐
☐

Calls to Make

Errands

Happen

Project

- ☐
- ☐
- ☐
- ☐
- ☐
- ☐
- ☐

Other

- ☐
- ☐
- ☐
- ☐
- ☐
- ☐
- ☐

Menu

Monday

Tuesday

Wednesday

Thursday

Friday

Saturday

Sunday

November

S	M	T	W	T	F	S
				1	2	3
4	5	6	7	8	9	10
11	12	13	14	15	16	17
18	19	20	21	22	23	24
25	26	27	28	29	30	

Do

Weekly Affirmation: _____

Monday	Tuesday	Wednesday
Dinner:	Dinner:	Dinner:
Exercise:	Exercise:	Exercise:

Notes

Water

	1	2	3	4	5	6	7	8
M								
T								
W								
T								
F								
S								
S								

It ⟶

Thursday	Friday	Saturday

Dinner: Dinner:

Exercise: Exercise:

Sunday

Daily Habits

	M	T	W	T	F	S	S

Appointments

Monthly Review

Best

Accomplishments	Significant Events	What brought the most joy?

Worst

Biggest Challenges	Personal Struggles	Changes for Next Month

Truth:

How am I different?

Financial Tracker

Income	
Expenses	
Profit	
Tithe	
Savings	

Weight Tracker

	M	T	W	T	F
Week 1					
Week 2					
Week 3					
Week 4					
Week 5					

Books I Read

I am most proud of:

Ideas & inspiration for next month

A Month at a Glance

And now let us welcome the new year, full of things that never were.
Lydia Sweatt

Goals: Writing

Week 1: _____
Week 2: _____
Week 3: _____
Week 4: _____
Week 5: _____

Goals: Marketing

Week 1: _____
Week 2: _____
Week 3: _____
Week 4: _____
Week 5: _____

Goals: Craft

Week 1: _____
Week 2: _____
Week 3: _____
Week 4: _____
Week 5: _____

Goals: Other

Week 1: _____
Week 2: _____
Week 3: _____
Week 4: _____
Week 5: _____

Important Dates

_____
_____
_____
_____
_____

Things to Remember:

_____
_____
_____
_____
_____

I AM grateful FOR:

_____
_____
_____
_____

Favorite Writing Quote

December

Sunday	Monday	Tuesday	Wednesday
2	3	4	5
9	10	11	12
16	17	18	19
23	24	25	26
30	31		

2018 ◇◈◇

Thursday	Friday	Saturday	Notes
		1	
6	7	8	
13	14	15	
20	21	22	
27	28	29	

Daily

Monday

Verse

Reflection

Truth

Prayers

Tuesday

Verse

Reflection

Truth

Prayers

Wednesday

Verse

Reflection

Truth

Prayers

Thursday

Verse

Reflection

Truth

Prayers

Inspiration

Friday

Verse

Prayers

Reflection

Truth

Saturday

Verse

Prayers

Reflection

Truth

Sunday

Verse

Prayers

Reflection

Truth

What encouraged you this week?

What can you do to encourage someone else?

Make it

Writing

☐
☐
☐
☐
☐
☐
☐

Marketing

☐
☐
☐
☐
☐
☐
☐

Craft

☐
☐
☐
☐
☐
☐
☐

Calls to Make

Errands

Happen

Project

- ☐
- ☐
- ☐
- ☐
- ☐
- ☐
- ☐

Other

- ☐
- ☐
- ☐
- ☐
- ☐
- ☐

Menu

Monday
Tuesday
Wednesday
Thursday
Friday
Saturday
Sunday

December

S	M	T	W	T	F	S
						1
2	3	4	5	6	7	8
9	10	11	12	13	14	15
16	17	18	19	20	21	22
23	24	25	26	27	28	29
30	31					

Do

Weekly Affirmation: _____

Monday	Tuesday	Wednesday
Dinner:	Dinner:	Dinner:
Exercise:	Exercise:	Exercise:

Notes

Water

	1	2	3	4	5	6	7	8
M								
T								
W								
T								
F								
S								
S								

It

Thursday	Friday	Saturday

Sunday

Dinner:

Dinner:

Exercise:

Exercise:

Daily Habits	M	T	W	T	F	S	S

Appointments

Daily

Monday

Verse

Reflection

Truth

Prayers

Tuesday

Verse

Reflection

Truth

Prayers

Wednesday

Verse

Reflection

Truth

Prayers

Thursday

Verse

Reflection

Truth

Prayers

Inspiration

Friday

Verse

Reflection

Truth

Prayers

Saturday

Verse

Reflection

Truth

Prayers

Sunday

Verse

Reflection

Truth

Prayers

What encouraged you this week?

What can you do to encourage someone else?

Make it

Writing

- ☐
- ☐
- ☐
- ☐
- ☐
- ☐
- ☐

Marketing

- ☐
- ☐
- ☐
- ☐
- ☐
- ☐
- ☐

Craft

- ☐
- ☐
- ☐
- ☐
- ☐
- ☐
- ☐

Calls to Make

Errands

Happen

Project

- ☐
- ☐
- ☐
- ☐
- ☐
- ☐
- ☐

Other

- ☐
- ☐
- ☐
- ☐
- ☐
- ☐
- ☐

Menu

Monday	
Tuesday	
Wednesday	
Thursday	
Friday	
Saturday	
Sunday	

December

S	M	T	W	T	F	S
						1
2	3	4	5	6	7	8
9	10	11	12	13	14	15
16	17	18	19	20	21	22
23	24	25	26	27	28	29
30	31					

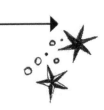

Do

Weekly Affirmation: _____

Monday	Tuesday	Wednesday
Dinner:	Dinner:	Dinner:
Exercise:	Exercise:	Exercise:

Notes

Water

	1	2	3	4	5	6	7	8
M								
T								
W								
T								
F								
S								
S								

It

Thursday	Friday	Saturday

Dinner:

Dinner:

Exercise:

Exercise:

Sunday

Daily Habits

	M	T	W	T	F	S	S

Appointments

Daily

Monday

Verse

Reflection

Truth

Prayers

Tuesday

Verse

Reflection

Truth

Prayers

Wednesday

Verse

Reflection

Truth

Prayers

Thursday

Verse

Reflection

Truth

Prayers

Inspiration

Friday

Verse

Reflection

Truth

Prayers

Saturday

Verse

Reflection

Truth

Prayers

Sunday

Verse

Reflection

Truth

Prayers

What encouraged you this week?

What can you do to encourage someone else?

Make it

Writing

- [ ]
- [ ]
- [ ]
- [ ]
- [ ]
- [ ]
- [ ]

Marketing

- [ ]
- [ ]
- [ ]
- [ ]
- [ ]
- [ ]
- [ ]

Craft

- [ ]
- [ ]
- [ ]
- [ ]
- [ ]
- [ ]
- [ ]

Calls to Make

Errands

Happen

Project

- ☐
- ☐
- ☐
- ☐
- ☐
- ☐
- ☐

Other

- ☐
- ☐
- ☐
- ☐
- ☐
- ☐

Menu

Monday
Tuesday
Wednesday
Thursday
Friday
Saturday
Sunday

December

S	M	T	W	T	F	S
						1
2	3	4	5	6	7	8
9	10	11	12	13	14	15
16	17	18	19	20	21	22
23	24	25	26	27	28	29
30	31					

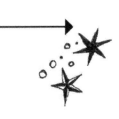

Do

Weekly Affirmation: _____

Monday	Tuesday	Wednesday
Dinner:	Dinner:	Dinner:
Exercise:	Exercise:	Exercise:

Notes

	1	2	3	4	5	6	7	8
M								
T								
W								
T								
F								
S								
S								

Water

It

Thursday	Friday	Saturday

Sunday

Dinner:

Dinner:

Exercise:

Exercise:

Daily Habits

	M	T	W	T	F	S	S

Appointments

Daily

Monday

Verse

Reflection

Truth

Prayers

Tuesday

Verse

Reflection

Truth

Prayers

Wednesday

Verse

Reflection

Truth

Prayers

Thursday

Verse

Reflection

Truth

Prayers

Inspiration

Friday

Verse

Reflection

Truth

Prayers

Saturday

Verse

Reflection

Truth

Prayers

Sunday

Verse

Reflection

Truth

Prayers

What encouraged you this week?

What can you do to encourage someone else?

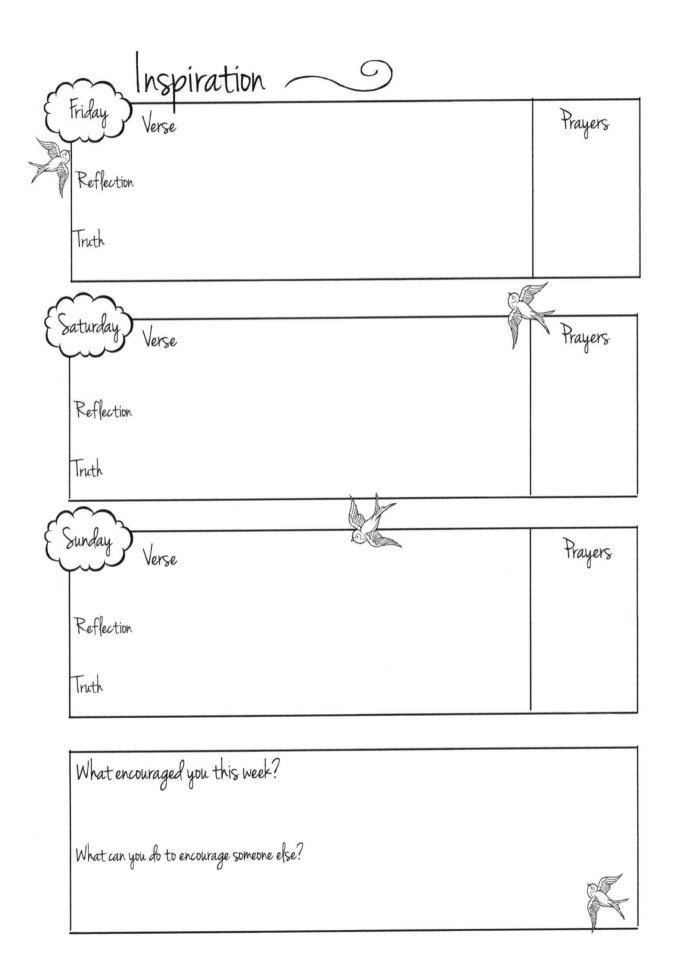

Make it

Writing	Marketing	Craft
☐	☐	☐
☐	☐	☐
☐	☐	☐
☐	☐	☐
☐	☐	☐
☐	☐	☐
☐	☐	☐

Calls to Make

Errands

Happen

Project

- ☐
- ☐
- ☐
- ☐
- ☐
- ☐
- ☐

Other

- ☐
- ☐
- ☐
- ☐
- ☐
- ☐

Menu

Monday	
Tuesday	
Wednesday	
Thursday	
Friday	
Saturday	
Sunday	

December

S	M	T	W	T	F	S
						1
2	3	4	5	6	7	8
9	10	11	12	13	14	15
16	17	18	19	20	21	22
23	24	25	26	27	28	29
30	31					

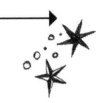

Do

Weekly Affirmation: _____

Monday	Tuesday	Wednesday
Dinner:	Dinner:	Dinner:
Exercise:	Exercise:	Exercise:

Notes

Water

	1	2	3	4	5	6	7	8
M								
T								
W								
T								
F								
S								
S								

It

Thursday	Friday	Saturday

Sunday

Dinner:

Dinner:

Exercise:

Exercise:

Daily Habits		M	T	W	T	F	S	S

Appointments

Daily

Monday

Verse

Reflection

Truth

Prayers

Tuesday

Verse

Reflection

Truth

Prayers

Wednesday

Verse

Reflection

Truth

Prayers

Thursday

Verse

Reflection

Truth

Prayers

Inspiration

Friday

Verse

Reflection

Truth

Prayers

Saturday

Verse

Reflection

Truth

Prayers

Sunday

Verse

Reflection

Truth

Prayers

What encouraged you this week?

What can you do to encourage someone else?

Make it

Writing

- ☐
- ☐
- ☐
- ☐
- ☐
- ☐
- ☐

Marketing

- ☐
- ☐
- ☐
- ☐
- ☐
- ☐
- ☐

Craft

- ☐
- ☐
- ☐
- ☐
- ☐
- ☐
- ☐

Calls to Make

Errands

Happen

Project

- ☐
- ☐
- ☐
- ☐
- ☐
- ☐
- ☐

Other

- ☐
- ☐
- ☐
- ☐
- ☐
- ☐

Menu

Monday
Tuesday
Wednesday
Thursday
Friday
Saturday
Sunday

December

S	M	T	W	T	F	S
						1
2	3	4	5	6	7	8
9	10	11	12	13	14	15
16	17	18	19	20	21	22
23	24	25	26	27	28	29
30	31					

Do

Weekly Affirmation: _____

Monday	Tuesday	Wednesday
Dinner:	Dinner:	Dinner:
Exercise:	Exercise:	Exercise:

Notes

Water

	1	2	3	4	5	6	7	8
M								
T								
W								
T								
F								
S								
S								

It

Thursday	Friday	Saturday

Sunday

Dinner:

Dinner:

Exercise:

Exercise:

Daily Habits

	M	T	W	T	F	S	S

Appointments

Monthly Review

Best

Accomplishments	Significant Events	What brought the most joy?

Worst

Biggest Challenges	Personal Struggles	Changes for Next Month

Truth:

How am I different?

Financial Tracker

Income	
Expenses	
Profit	
Tithe	
Savings	

Weight Tracker

	M	T	W	T	F
Week 1					
Week 2					
Week 3					
Week 4					
Week 5					

Books I Read

I am most proud of:

Ideas & inspiration for next month

Year End Review

Activites/Projects/Events that brought joy!

Challenges

Hopes for next year

Summary of last year, things I learned, things I loved, truths and ways God showed up!

❊❊❊ January 2019 ❊❊❊

Sunday	Monday	Tuesday	Wednesday	Thursday	Friday	Saturday
		1	2	3	4	5
6	7	8	9	10	11	12
13	14	15	16	17	18	19
20	21	22	23	24	25	26
27	28	29	30	31		

January

S	M	T	W	T	F	S
		1	2	3	4	5
6	7	8	9	10	11	12
13	14	15	16	17	18	19
20	21	22	23	24	25	26
27	28	29	30	31		

Dates to remember:

February

S	M	T	W	T	F	S
					1	2
3	4	5	6	7	8	9
10	11	12	13	14	15	16
17	18	19	20	21	22	23
24	25	26	27	28		

Dates to remember:

March

S	M	T	W	T	F	S
					1	2
3	4	5	6	7	8	9
10	11	12	13	14	15	16
17	18	19	20	21	22	23
24	25	26	27	28	29	30
31						

Dates to remember:

July

S	M	T	W	T	F	S
	1	2	3	4	5	6
7	8	9	10	11	12	13
14	15	16	17	18	19	20
21	22	23	24	25	26	27
28	29	30	31			

Dates to remember:

August

S	M	T	W	T	F	S
				1	2	3
4	5	6	7	8	9	10
11	12	13	14	15	16	17
18	19	20	21	22	23	24
25	26	27	28	29	30	31

Dates to remember:

September

S	M	T	W	T	F	S
1	2	3	4	5	6	7
8	9	10	11	12	13	14
15	16	17	18	19	20	21
22	23	24	25	26	27	28
29	30					

Dates to remember:

Color code your events

☐ birthdays ☐ anniversaries ☐ holidays ☐ vacations

2019

April

S	M	T	W	T	F	S
	1	2	3	4	5	6
7	8	9	10	11	12	13
14	15	16	17	18	19	20
21	22	23	24	25	26	27
28	29	30				

Dates to remember:

May

S	M	T	W	T	F	S
			1	2	3	4
5	6	7	8	9	10	11
12	13	14	15	16	17	18
19	20	21	22	23	24	25
26	27	28	29	30	31	

Dates to remember:

June

S	M	T	W	T	F	S
						1
2	3	4	5	6	7	8
9	10	11	12	13	14	15
16	17	18	19	20	21	22
23	24	25	26	27	28	29
30						

Dates to remember:

October

S	M	T	W	T	F	S
		1	2	3	4	5
6	7	8	9	10	11	12
13	14	15	16	17	18	19
20	21	22	23	24	25	26
27	28	29	30	31		

Dates to remember:

November

S	M	T	W	T	F	S
					1	2
3	4	5	6	7	8	9
10	11	12	13	14	15	16
17	18	19	20	21	22	23
24	25	26	27	28	29	30

Dates to remember:

December

S	M	T	W	T	F	S
1	2	3	4	5	6	7
8	9	10	11	12	13	14
15	16	17	18	19	20	21
22	23	24	25	26	27	28
29	30	31				

Dates to remember:

Color code your events

☐ conferences ☐ deadlines ☐ pub dates ☐ projects

Motivational Quotes

To begin, begin. ~ William Wordsworth

Life is 10 % what happens to you and 90 % how you react to it. ~ Charles R. Swindoll

In order to succeed, we must first believe that we can. ~ Nikos Kazantzakis

The secret of getting ahead is getting started. ~ Mark Twain

If you can dream it, you can do it. ~ Walt Disney

Keep your eyes on the stars, and your feet on the ground. ~ Theodore Roosevelt

Accept the challenges so that you can feel the exhilaration of victory. ~ George S. Patton

Quality is not an act, it is a habit. ~ Aristotle

Never, never, never give up. ~ Winston Churchill

Problems are not stop signs, they are guidelines. ~ Robert H. Schuller

You are never too old to set another goal or to dream a new dream. ~ Les Brown

Without hard work, nothing grows but weeds. ~ Gordon B. Hinckley

The harder the conflict, the more glorious the triumph. ~ Thomas Paine

There is no passion to be found playing small - in settling for a life that is less than the one you are capable of living. ~ Nelson Mandela

I'd rather attempt to do something great and fail than to attempt to do nothing and succeed. ~ Robert H. Schuller

Act as if what you do makes a difference. It does. ~ William James

Perseverance is failing 19 times and succeeding the 20th. ~ Julie Andrews

The most effective way to do it, is to do it. ~ Amelia Earhart

You will never win if you never begin. ~ Helen Rowland

We aim above the mark to hit the mark. ~ Ralph Waldo Emerson

Go for it now. The future is promised to no one. ~ Wayne Dyer

Wherever you are - be all there. ~ Jim Elliot

Do something wonderful, people may imitate it. ~ Albert Schweitzer

I am not afraid... I was born to do this. ~ Joan of Arc

It's always too early to quit. ~ Norman Vincent Peale

I attribute my success to this - I never gave or took any excuse. ~ Florence Nightingale

You just can't beat the person who never gives up. ~ Babe Ruth

A goal is a dream with a deadline. ~ Napoleon Hill

You can't wait for inspiration. You have to go after it with a club. ~ Jack London

I am not a has-been. I am a will be. ~ Lauren Bacall

Storycrafting

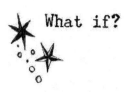

What if?

Possible Titles

Premise

who

wants

what

why

or else

so

but

black moment event

epiphany/lesson learned

Urgency

Stakes

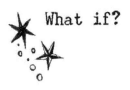 What if?

Possible Titles

Premise

who

wants

what

why

or else

so

but

black moment event

epiphany/lesson learned

Urgency

Stakes

Character SEQ: (name)

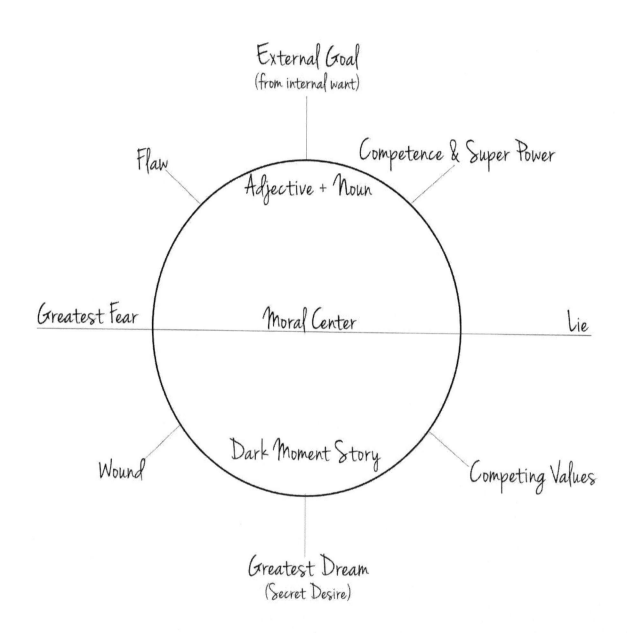

External Goal
(from internal want)

Competence & Super Power

Flaw

Adjective + Noun

Greatest Fear

Moral Center

Lie

Wound

Dark Moment Story

Competing Values

Greatest Dream
(Secret Desire)

Character SEQ: (name)

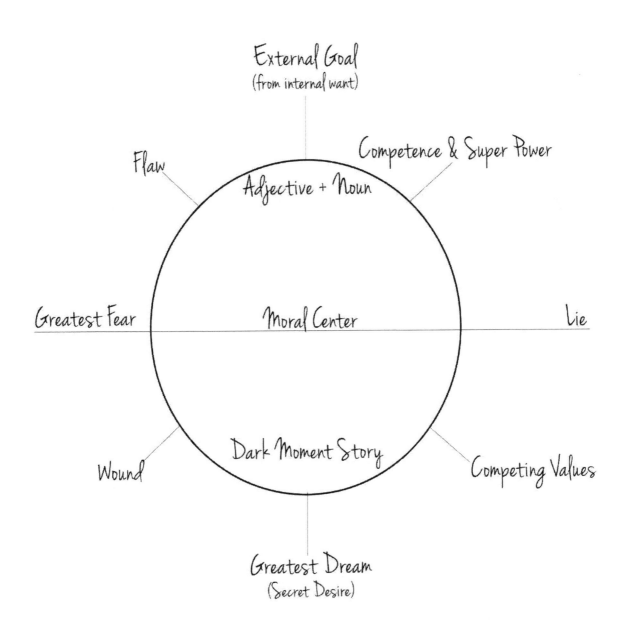

External Goal
(from internal want)

Competence & Super Power

Flaw

Adjective + Noun

Greatest Fear

Moral Center

Lie

Dark Moment Story

Wound

Competing Values

Greatest Dream
(Secret Desire)

Rough Story Plot

Act 1

Life

Inciting Incident

  Great Debate

Noble Quest

Life
Inciting Incident
Great Debate
Noble Quest

Act 2 A

Attempt

Cost

Reward

Attempt

Desire

Attempt

Cost

Reward

Attempt

Desire

Act 2 B

MIM

D-Y

D-Y

D-Y

Black Moment Event

D-Y

D-Y

D-Y

Black Moment Event

Act 3

Black Moment Effect
Epiphany

Final Battle

Perfect Ending

Black Moment Effect
Epiphany

Final Battle

Perfect Ending

Indie Production Planning Sheet

Series Name

Title	RD Date	Macro	Micro	Proofing	Preorder	Pub Date

Logline/Pitch

Premise

Endorsers

.

Marketing costs	Facebk	AMS Ads	Mailers	Book Bub	Other	Total
Budget						
Editorial costs	Macro	Micro	Proofing	VA	Other	Total
Budget						
Cover costs					Total	
Layout costs					Total	
Other costs					Total	

Total Costs of Production	
Price per book	
Earn out number*	

Take the total costs and divide it by the price per book

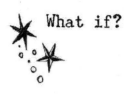

What if?

Possible Titles

Premise

who

wants

what

why

or else

so

but

black moment event

epiphany/lesson learned

Urgency

Stakes

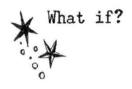

What if?

Possible Titles

Premise
who

wants

what

why

or else

so

but

black moment event

epiphany/lesson learned

Urgency

Stakes

Character SEQ: (name)

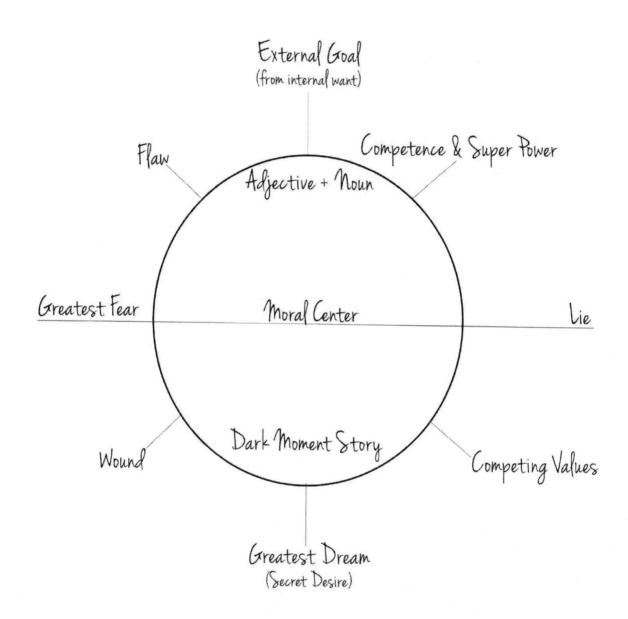

Character SEQ: (name)

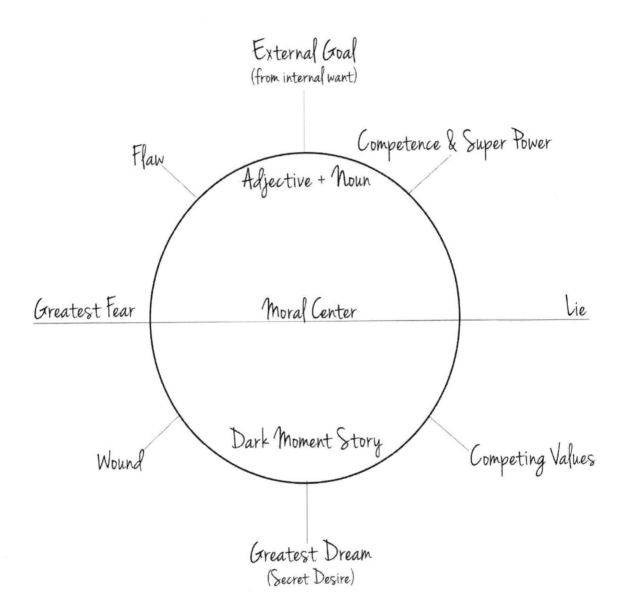

External Goal
(from internal want)

Competence & Super Power

Flaw

Adjective + Noun

Greatest Fear

Moral Center

Lie

Wound

Dark Moment Story

Competing Values

Greatest Dream
(Secret Desire)

Rough Story Plot

Act 1

Life

Inciting Incident

Great Debate

Noble Quest

Life

Inciting Incident

Great Debate

Noble Quest

Act 2 A

Attempt

Cost

Reward

Attempt

Desire

Attempt

Cost

Reward

Attempt

Desire

Act 2 B

MIM

D-Y

D-Y

D-Y

Black Moment Event

D-Y

D-Y

D-Y

Black Moment Event

Act 3

Black Moment Effect
Epiphany

Final Battle

Perfect Ending

Black Moment Effect
Epiphany

Final Battle

Perfect Ending

Indie Production Planning Sheet

Series Name

Title	RD Date	Macro	Micro	Proofing	Preorder	Pub Date

Logline/Pitch

Premise

Endorsers

Marketing costs	Facebk	AMS Ads	Mailers	Book Bub	Other	Total
Budget						
Editorial costs	Macro	Micro	Proofing	VA	Other	Total
Budget						
Cover costs					Total	
Layout costs					Total	
Other costs					Total	
				Total Costs of Production		
				Price per book		
				Earn out number*		

Take the total costs and divide it by the price per book

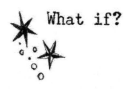 What if?

Possible Titles

Premise

who

wants

what

why

or else

so

but

black moment event

epiphany/lesson learned

Urgency

Stakes

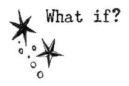

What if?

Possible Titles

Premise

who

wants

what

why

or else

so

but

black moment event

epiphany/lesson learned

Urgency

Stakes

Character SEQ: (name)

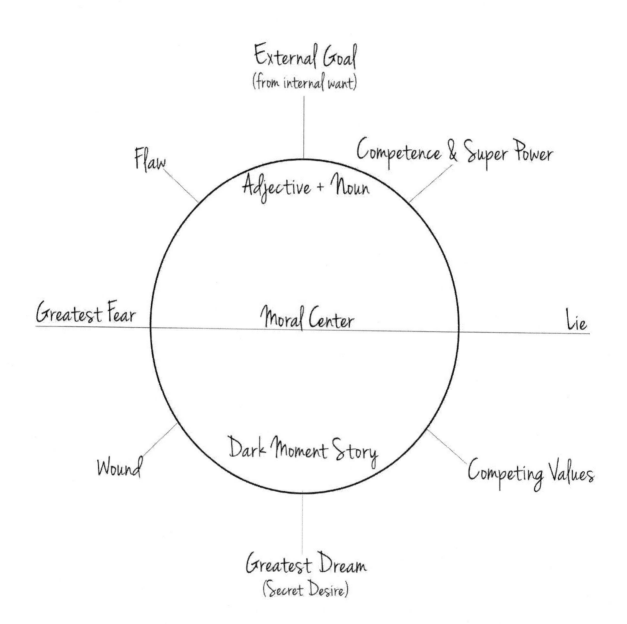

External Goal
(from internal want)

Competence & Super Power

Flaw

Adjective + Noun

Greatest Fear

Moral Center

Lie

Wound

Dark Moment Story

Competing Values

Greatest Dream
(Secret Desire)

Character SEQ: (name)

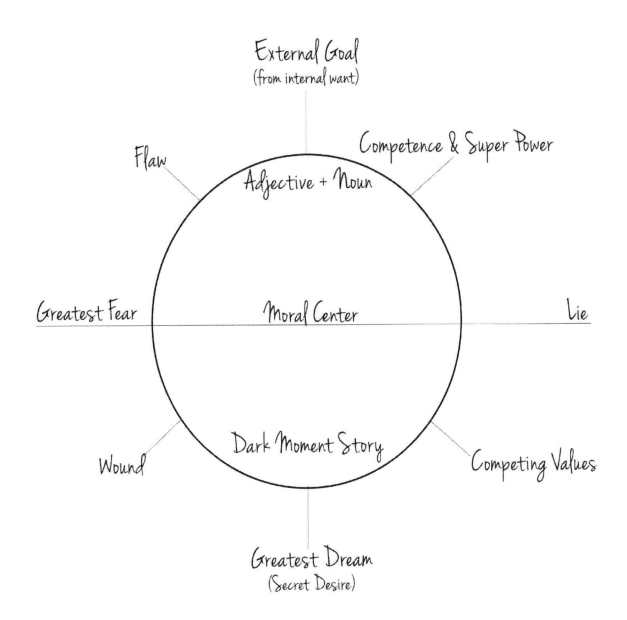

External Goal
(from internal want)

Competence & Super Power

Flaw

Adjective + Noun

Greatest Fear

Moral Center

Lie

Wound

Dark Moment Story

Competing Values

Greatest Dream
(Secret Desire)

Rough Story Plot

Act 1

Life

Inciting Incident

Great Debate

Noble Quest

Life

Inciting Incident

Great Debate

Noble Quest

Act 2 A

Attempt

Cost

Reward

Attempt

Desire

Attempt

Cost

Reward

Attempt

Desire

Act 2 B

MIM

D-y

D-y

D-y

Black Moment Event

D-y

D-y

D-y

Black Moment Event

Act 3

Black Moment Effect
Epiphany

Final Battle

Perfect Ending

Black Moment Effect
Epiphany

Final Battle

Perfect Ending

Indie Production Planning Sheet

Series Name _____

Title	RD Date	Macro	Micro	Proofing	Preorder	Pub Date

Logline/Pitch

Premise

Endorsers

Marketing costs	Facebk	AMS Ads	Mailers	Book Bub	Other	Total
Budget						

Editorial costs	Macro	Micro	Proofing	VA	Other	Total
Budget						

Cover costs				Total	
Layout costs				Total	
Other costs				Total	

Total Costs of Production	
Price per book	
Earn out number*	

Take the total costs and divide it by the price per book

Made in the USA
Lexington, KY
28 December 2017